The MEMORY Workbook

Mark Channon

To Zoë – you had me at the loop – and my three superheroes, Zachery, Elijah and Noah

Mark Channon, creator of the BBC1 gameshow *Memory Masters*, originally trained as an actor before becoming one of the first eight people in the world to become a Grand Master of Memory in the 1995 World Memory Championships. He has worked as a trainer for over 15 years, running seminars on memory and accelerated learning for organizations such as Rothschild, Lincoln National, the Institute of Chartered Accountants for England and Wales, Dyslexia Scotland and the BBC. As an executive coach, Mark works with clients to help them learn more effectively, grow their skills and achieve results in their career. He is also the author of *Teach Yourself How To Remember Anything* (2011).

The MEMORY Workbook

Mark Channon

Teach Yourself®

First published in Great Britain in 2013 by Hodder & Stoughton. An Hachette UK company.

First published in US in 2013 by The McGraw-Hill Companies, Inc.

This edition published 2013

British Library Cataloguing in Publication Data: a catalogue record for this title is available from the British Library.

Library of Congress Catalog Card Number: on file.

10 9 8 7 6 5 4 3 2 1

The publisher has used its best endeavours to ensure that any website addresses referred to in this book are correct and active at the time of going to press. However, the publisher and the author have no responsibility for the websites and can make no guarantee that a site will remain live or that the content will remain relevant, decent or appropriate.

The publisher has made every effort to mark as such all words which it believes to be trademarks. The publisher should also like to make it clear that the presence of a word in the book, whether marked or unmarked, in no way affects its legal status as a trademark.

Every reasonable effort has been made by the publisher to trace the copyright holders of material in this book. Any errors or omissions should be notified in writing to the publisher, who will endeavour to rectify the situation for any reprints and future editions.

Cover image © freshidea/fotolia

Typeset by Cenveo® Publisher Services.

Printed and bound in Great Britain by CPI Group (UK) Ltd, Croydon CRO 4YY.

Hodder & Stoughton policy is to use papers that are natural, renewable and recyclable products and made from wood grown in sustainable forests. The logging and manufacturing processes are expected to conform to the environmental regulations of the country of origin.

Hodder & Stoughton Ltd
338 Euston Road
London NW1 3BH
www.hodder.co.uk

Acknowledgements

My thanks to Victoria Roddam, Sarah Chapman and everyone at Hodder & Stoughton for giving me the opportunity to write my second book; to the staff at Costa in Sevenoaks for all the cappuccinos; to Jennifer Goddard for offering photos from the World Memory Championships; to Phillip Ash for his mind map contribution; to Dominic McHale for always being around; and to Richard Lyon – you know why. Thanks to Sally and Ed for your support, and to Mum, Dad and brothers John and Paul, who offered inspiration at different times throughout the writing of this book.

Special thanks to Zoë for all your work, and for keeping me straight and on target; you're the best.

Contents

How to use this book

This workbook from Teach Yourself ® includes a number of special features which have been developed to help you understand the subject more quickly and reach your goal successfully. Throughout the book, you will find these indicated by the following icons.

 Key ideas: to make sure you grasp the most important points.

 Spotlight: an important and useful definition explained in more depth.

 Exercise: designed to help you to work out where you are, where you want to be and how to achieve your goals. Exercises include:

 writing exercises - fill in your answers in the space provided.

 reflective exercises - think about the way you do things.

 Dig deeper: an exercise that offers further reflection or deeper explanations of the topic.

 Test yourself: assess yourself with multiple-choice questions or multiple selections.

 Practice: put the ideas you learn about into practice.

 Quotes: inspiring and motivating you.

At the end of each chapter you will find:

 Summary: a section consolidating the main things you should remember from that chapter.

 What I have learned: helping you summarize for yourself what you can take away from each chapter.

 Where to next?: introducing you to the next step.

Introduction

In this introduction you will learn about:
▶ the real-life benefits of a better memory
▶ the process described in this workbook
▶ the challenging activities that will track your progress.

Most of us take our memory for granted. We generally don't think about the fact that we remember how to make breakfast, ride a bike or drive a car; we just 'know these things'. We have conversations with our family about our day at work; we reminisce when we meet old friends. We make decisions day by day, based on the memories of our past experiences. A past relationship that ended badly may affect a person getting into a new relationship. A child, having experienced the thrill of being on stage, is spurred on years later to look for a career in a highly unstable yet ultimately rewarding profession.

We only tend to notice how important memory truly is when we forget 'the speech' or try to recall the right answers during an exam, when we are learning new skills for a new job or experiencing the stress that can come with information overload and 'getting it into our head'. Perhaps we first notice its importance when we see others starting to lose the type of memory ability we take for granted. In this sense, our memories make us what we are.

→ Journey to a better memory

Back in 1993 I got involved in the world of memory techniques. Around a year later, I received a phone call from my agent asking whether I had any ideas for a new game show. This led me to create a show called *Memory Masters*, which was aired on TV within 12 months. Shortly afterwards, I competed in the World Memory Championships, ranking third in the world as a Grand Master of Memory. This was an exciting time, but it wasn't until I started working with people on a much wider basis that my view of memory techniques changed dramatically.

In the beginning, mnemonics felt like a bunch of really cool tricks, but as I worked with more and more people and built my own skill set, I realized that this creative way of memorizing and learning skills that you could use, put into practice and get some very significant results from was really a *way of thinking*. For most people, conditioned to learn in a linear, repetitious manner, it was a completely *new way of thinking* and one that required effort.

It was during my early experiences as a memory trainer that I remember two different participants in a workshop, Helen and Jenny. Jenny was studying acupuncture and Helen just wanted some general improvements to her memory. Shortly after the workshop, I received a letter from each of them.

Jenny talked about how she had previously failed an acupuncture exam three times and then, having attended the memory workshop, managed to pass with full marks. This sounded great and started to confirm my beliefs that these strategies were exceedingly underused in our society. The second letter from Helen was even more revealing and surprising to me, as it talked about a major increase in confidence, how it had changed her life and about how she now felt she could study and do anything she wanted.

Reading it, I remember thinking, 'But these are just a bunch of tricks!' Then I started to realize that their impact went much further. It began to make sense to me that having the ability to remember confidently and living this new belief was significant, and it dawned on me that these so-called tricks had acted as a catalyst for these participants. Essentially, they had both had an experience that gave them a new set of memories that changed how they thought about themselves and that would potentially affect their future decisions and choices.

This revelation has ultimately led me to the writing of *The Memory Workbook*, many years later. This is your practical guide to:

• improving your memory

• discovering the real benefits that an excellent memory can deliver

• keeping your memory in great shape

• learning to tap into your innate set of skills that will make you feel sharper

• accelerating your ability to learn.

→ Learn – grow – achieve

By putting in the right amount of effort and working through the exercises in this workbook, you will accelerate your learning, enhancing your skills and knowledge to achieve great results in all areas of your life. Whether you are aiming to pass an exam, learn how to dance, gain skills for a new job, teach a family member or simply increase your confidence, you will find the techniques here invaluable. We will use Howard Gardner's theory of multiple intelligences as the lens to view how a better, more powerful memory can add real value to your life and help you perform smarter with words, numbers, music, pictures, body and emotions (your own and other people's).

At the core of this book are some basic ideas:

▶ Learning is about creating.

▶ Growing comes from learning.

▶ Achievements are a result of your growth.

The workbook covers these themes as follows:

LEARN

Chapters 3–5 are your personal toolbox. The exercises will accelerate your ability to remember, comprehend, put into practice and master key mental states that will allow you to achieve your goals and get results.

GROW

Chapters 6–11 contain exercises that will help you improve your knowledge and skills in order to become smarter in seven key areas of intelligence. This section of the workbook isn't so much about increasing your intelligence per se as it is about gaining the 'edge' by using creative memorization to improve performance.

ACHIEVE

Chapters 12 and 13 will help you get clarity on your goals, and create a strategy and a plan for how to get where you want to be. The exercises will show you how to 'chunk it up', monitor and measure your success, and become more flexible and adaptable as you achieve your aims.

By the end of this workbook you will have learned how to work 'smarter' and give yourself the edge when it comes to your memory.

→ Seven steps to smarter

1 Before doing anything else, take no more than five minutes to preview this book. Read the index, flick through page by page and acknowledge areas that grab your attention. **Important:** do not read in any detail!

2 Once you have previewed, take a piece of A4 paper and answer the following five questions – stick the answers on a wall or a whiteboard if you have one, feel free to draw pictures which represent your answers and then talk it through out loud or talk someone else through what you are about to do:

▶ What do I think this book will give me?

▶ How will what I learn make a difference in my life?

▶ What will I have achieved six months after living with the skills I have used in this workbook?

▶ How committed am I to finishing this workbook on a scale of one to ten?

▶ If I am below eight, what will it take to get to eight or above?

3 Spend 10–20 minutes skimming through the book at high speed (resist the temptation to do any of the activities). Do not worry about remembering any detail; just get a sense of what the book will be giving you.

4 Probe – spend ten minutes with a whiteboard or a large sheet of paper and some coloured pens, noting down what you think the book is about, adding more details as to what it will give you, and how you will use it.

5 Allocate yourself a set amount of time daily or weekly, ideally 30 minutes per session. The length of time to complete a chapter will vary from person to person.

6 Work through the chapters in order up to the end of Chapter 5, on accelerated learning.

7 For the 'smarts' chapters (6–11), you can do them in the order you prefer.

→ Track your progress

Within this workbook are more than 100 exercises designed to diagnose where you are, enhance your skills, accelerate your learning, boost your memory and create the momentum to achieve the results you want.

▶ Each exercise is worth one point.

▶ There are a total of 104 points in this book.

HOW IT WORKS

After you complete each exercise, use a highlighter pen to shade in the cell in the table below.

1. The right mindset	2. Memory checklist	3. Visualizing your ideal scene	4. Your world map: goals	5. Your world map: challenges
6. Your world map: skills, knowledge and feelings	7. The rocking chair technique	8. Becoming aware	9. Your episodic memory	10. Your semantic memory
11. Your procedural memory	12. Priming your brain	13. Your conditioned responses	14. Your emotional memory	15. Your working memory
16. Supporting your memory	17. Benchmarking your progress	18. The 100 billion	19. Creating flow	20. Creating metaphors
21. Test your memorization skills	22. Creating reference stories	23. Dialling up	24. Remote control	25. Using sense memory
26. Using emotional recall	27. Using your iMind	28. Chain reaction	29. Creative chains	30. The 125 test
31. Increasing your rhythm	32. Using the body system	33. The memory palace	34. The journey system	35. Limitless
36. Real-life applications	37. The learning cycle	38. Identifying your learning style	39. Designing your learning	40. Memory smarts
41. Performing	42. Your map of words	43. Emotive words	44. A word journal	45. Get the root
46. Business terms	47. Learning another language	48. Storyboards	49. Using quotes	50. Test your number memory
51. Where are you with numbers?	52. Remembering numbers: the basics	53. Creating a language for numbers	54. Using sound cards	55. Breaking the code
56. Learning your memory matrix	57. Memorizing extension numbers	58. Memorizing PINs and bank cards	59. Memorizing statistics	60. Remembering dates
61. Exploring your musical experience	62. What's your musical intelligence?	63. Honing your musical ear	64. Using music trigger words	65. Tapping it out
66. Musical moves	67. Mapping music networks	68. Memorizing playlists	69. Remembering the top tracks	70. Mapping your visual memory

71. Discovering your inner artist	72. Using visual thinking	73. Pitching with a mind map	74. How do I get to...?	75. Brain flow
76. Using memory tags	77. Creating memory triggers	78. Mapping your physical ability	79. Targets and rewards	80. Metaphor moves
81. Absorbing anatomy terms	82. Visual cues	83. Sequencing	84. Memorizing keyboard shortcuts	85. Coffee time
86. Sit up!	87. Mapping your emotional intelligence	88. Growing pains	89. Creating future memories	90. Releasing anxiety
91. Names and you	92. Meeting the team	93. Creative listening	94. Having a creative conversation	95. Whose round?
96. Warm-ups	97. Speed games	98. Stamina games	99. The speech	100. Bringing variety to your workout
101. Creating your timeline	102. Memory and your values	103. Memory beliefs	104. Your final challenge	

THE MEMORY CHART

Next, use a memory burnup chart to visualize your progress. Download the chart from www.achieve-with.me/memoryworkbook

1 Stick it on a wall!

2 Count up the total points you have completed at the end of each day.

3 Make a mark on the chart.

4 Draw a line from yesterday to today.

This is a simple and easy way not only to track your progress but also to offer yourself daily rewards or motivators for the number of points you work through.

The Memory Workbook Facebook group

Finally, join the Facebook group for this workbook – a community of people improving their memory and achieving results. As you go through this workbook, use it to ask questions, get help, and share your challenges and successes. This is a secret Facebook group, meaning that only members can see who's in the group and post. It's a growing community where you can get advice and tips as you progress through the workbook. You also get priority invitations to free webinars with Mark Channon Coaching, offering first-hand advice on improving your skills.

http://www.facebook.com/groups/memoryworkbook

Summary

So far, you have discovered the benefits of a better memory, the seven steps you need to take in order to achieve it, and that the way to learn how to motivate yourself is through targets and progress tracking, as set out in the following chapters. Through them, you'll create a programme that plays to your strengths. You are about to embark on a fun and exciting journey that can deliver some powerful rewards. Enjoy!

What I have learned

What are my thoughts, feelings and insights on what I have read so far?

_____

_____

_____

Use the space below to summarize the actions to take as a result of reading this introduction.

_____

_____

_____

_____

Where to next?

By now it should be clear: engage with the exercises in this workbook and your memory will improve. Allow yourself the opportunity to learn.

In Chapter 1 we will identify the key drivers that make you want to improve your memory. We'll also explore just how great an impact a powerful memory can have on all aspects of your life and start setting goals that will achieve real results.

1 Get results!

In this chapter you will learn:
- ▶ to identify the key drivers that make you want to improve your memory
- ▶ how a powerful memory can make an impact on your life
- ▶ to create goals that focus on real-life results.

As you begin this invigorating journey into the world of memory, what happens when you think about your destination? How much clarity do you have in terms of where you are going? Can you describe it in detail? Is it compelling enough to keep you motivated when there are difficult challenges ahead? Is this something that must happen for you or is it merely something that would be nice to have?

During this exploration, you will discover some of your key strengths and weaknesses, where you excel and what you need to work on. Whatever challenges you face, having a positive mindset will help drive you forward, learning as you go, growing your knowledge and putting your new skills into practice.

In this chapter you are going to employ some effective visual thinking strategies to create that mindset. They will give you the level of momentum you need to motivate yourself towards your goal, by giving you an understanding of why a great memory is a good thing – not for anyone else, but for you.

> '*Nothing will come of nothing.*'
>
> William Shakespeare

Exercise 1

 THE RIGHT MINDSET

This exercise asks you to think about the characteristics you would need to have, in your approach to this book, in order to get the best results.

While thinking about your own personality, choose a persona below that most closely matches you, in terms of your approach to new skills and knowledge.

1 Dave the Dabbler	2 Suzy the Stressor	3 Mike the Master
Dave gets passionate about new things, he loves variety and big-picture thinking and, when he follows through, he can achieve good results. The challenge is not to get distracted and set off on a different journey before completing the one he is on.	Suzy works really hard, and won't just do things once but over and over again until she feels she has got them done right. She feels she must know everything before she feels comfortable using it. She can get good results but it can sometimes feel like a stressful journey.	Mike knows where he wants to go, enjoys the journey and will usually have a map showing which direction to go in. He 'goes with the flow' and accepts that he won't get everything right and may have to alter his destination. He keeps going until he makes it to where he wants to be and is always looking to grow and find new adventures.

How easy would the persona you matched most closely find it to go through this workbook and put things into practice in a valuable way? Do you already have these characteristics? Are there any that could slow you down or get in your way?

What would be the **ideal persona** to adopt during this workbook? Is it one of the above, a mixture, or something new?

→ Create your ideal persona below; draw a picture and describe their characteristics and their approach to new skills and knowledge.

Refer back to this persona during the weeks ahead, as a reminder of the attitudes and approach you are going to use during the course of this workbook.

Adopt this persona's characteristics while using this workbook!

→ Why improve your memory?

How many people have you met who say they would love to have a better memory? I expect there are quite a few. The fact that you are reading this workbook says that you are somewhere on a scale of interested or highly committed to achieving that same goal.

How many of those same people you know are unwilling to invest the amount of effort it requires to take their memory to a new level? In the same way that there are no magic bullets or pills that will knock you up a six-pack in four weeks or get you rich quick, there are no magic bullets or pills that will turn you into a memory machine. Achievements like these all take effort, especially in the beginning. However, over time this effort brings rewards.

There is a general view that, if you exercise regularly, the benefits will include better health and increased energy, which can in turn improve performance in other areas of your life. The same goes for keeping yourself mentally healthy: with this kind of training also come increased energy and performance benefits.

With anything you attempt to learn in life, there is a certain amount of effort used or energy brought to it. The value you get from that effort has to be, at least in the medium to long term, worth that effort. Some things take longer than others to see their value. If you ever played tennis, for example, you will remember that in the beginning there was a lot of effort and you may have 'failed' (hit the net) most of the time, but when it did go over, that small reward spurred you on to continue and – as your skill grew – it became more fun. Of course, you may well have had the opposite experience, where your hand–eye co-ordination wasn't up to it and you just kept hitting the net. There were no rewards, just lots of effort, and even though you knew that, if you practised for long enough you might get there, it just didn't feel 'worth it'.

Learning how to learn may be similar to one of these experiences, so it is important that you first understand the long-term benefits you are trying to gain and the cost of what not having those will look and feel like for you, as well as how things will turn out when you incorporate this way of thinking into how you operate. In the short term you have to have rewards, those smaller successes that pull you forward, get you excited about the possibilities, while at the same time not getting disheartened because you haven't gone as far as you would like.

If you have ever crammed for an exam or worked through the night to deliver something the next day, you will know what **important** and **urgent** feel like. You will also instinctively know that important is sometimes not enough:

▶ 'I'll start the new healthy living on Monday.'
▶ 'I will read that book next week.'

It is the feeling of *urgency* that can call us to action. While you may want to avoid the feelings of anxiety associated with a sense of urgency, having just the right cocktail of 'goals, benefits, reward, importance and urgency' can be the difference between stopping a workbook like this three or four chapters in or flying through to the end, getting it 'into your body' and achieving results that can add value to your personal or professional life.

What is the right mix for you? What are the reasons you already know of that would make having a better memory not just important for you now but also urgent?

Exercise 2

MEMORY CHECKLIST

Think about some of the reasons that made you want to improve your memory. Go through the following checklist and tick the reasons that you think fit your situation and add any others specific to you.

Personal

Grow my knowledge and skills ☐
Accelerate learning ☐
Improve comprehension of new material ☐
Hold more information to solve problems ☐
Remember names, details, talks and facts ☐
Be in control of my time (less forgetting) ☐
Increase my confidence ☐
Pass tests and exams ☐
Help my kids through school ☐
Unleash my creative skills ☐
Speak up with confidence ☐
Learn a physical activity (dance, martial arts) ☐
Reduce stress and anxiety (fear of forgetting) ☐
Keep my brain fit (feeling sharper, alert) ☐
_____ ☐
_____ ☐
_____ ☐
_____ ☐
_____ ☐

Professional

Deal with information overload ☐
Remember key information at interviews ☐
Improve my work performance ☐
Demonstrate key facts in meetings ☐
Remember clients and customers ☐
Keep on top of market data and research ☐
Stay on top of product/service information ☐
Master new processes ☐
Train for a new career ☐
Influence with evidence ☐
Be known as the expert in my area ☐
Increase my earning potential ☐
Help my students (if you teach) ☐
Improve my team's performance ☐
_____ ☐
_____ ☐
_____ ☐
_____ ☐
_____ ☐

Exercise 3

VISUALIZING YOUR IDEAL SCENE

When you think about having a better memory, what does your ideal scene look like? If you could achieve any or all of the items on your memory checklist in the previous exercise, what difference would this make for you? Simply visualize the scene in your mind.

Now take a moment and imagine yourself at some point in the future, having lived out all the benefits you have ticked.

Get yourself into a comfortable position, breathe deeply and let yourself relax, notice where any tension is in your body and think, feel or see it melt away... Now imagine that you can wave a realistic magic wand that will allow you to learn anything, remember any piece of knowledge or master any skill.

➜ What impact might this have in the above areas?

_____

_____

➜ What results might you achieve?

_____

_____

Listen online: www.achieve-with.me/memoryworkbook

Imagine yourself in a room, a place that feels familiar to you, comfortable and full of opportunities. You can see a door in front of you and you feel excited to think about what adventures lie beyond that door... Slowly open the door and, as you open it, you can see a tunnel that stretches far into the distance. At the other end there is an opening. This opening takes you out to a time 12 months in your future...

As you stand here, feeling the ground beneath your feet, notice details of this tunnel and start to become aware of many windows along the tunnel walls. Behind those windows are exciting opportunities and new learning waiting for you to experience, which will bring value to many areas of your life.

In a moment, you will start to walk through the tunnel towards the opening… on your way you may catch glimpses of some of your future experiences as if they have already happened. Enjoy anything that you see, hear or feel…

Counting down from 12 to 1, start to walk through this tunnel, each number taking you further into the future towards the opening… relax and enjoy your journey… 12, 11, 10 enjoy any experiences that come to mind, 9, 8, 7, 6 notice how your confidence, skills and knowledge are growing on your journey, 5, 4, 3 in a moment you will arrive at your destination, 2, 1 notice your surroundings.

Where are you 12 months from now, having grown in key areas of your life?

➜ What have you achieved physically?

_____

➜ How do you feel emotionally?

_____

➜ What impact have you had on family, friends and colleagues?

_____

➜ How well are you making use of your time?

_____

➜ What results have you achieved in your career, business or mission in life?

_____

➜ What benefits have you experienced with your finances as a result of your skills?

_____

➜ What contributions are you making that wouldn't have been possible 12 months ago?

_____

Take some time and enjoy where you are... breathe deeply and relax... When you are ready, come back to the present in your own time.

→ Mapping your world

Think of Marmite. What are your thoughts? Whenever I ask this question to a roomful of people, there is usually a split between those who love it and those who hate it. Now think of mind maps.™ What are your thoughts? Again, whenever I ask this question to a room, similar splits tend to happen. If you believe you can't mind map or that mind maps are not useful, explore what is getting in your way. Perhaps you believe you can't draw, or that they are too complex? There can be many different reasons, but by following a few simple principles you can lower some of the barriers around mind mapping.

One of the major benefits of mind mapping is that it is a form of visual note-taking that allows you to work with many pieces of information at the same time, making it easier for your working memory to manipulate information and create connections.

Here is a simple way to create a mind map:

1 Begin with a centre that symbolizes your main thought.

2 From this centre, draw 'branches': think nature for your branches: a tree has a thick trunk and the branches get smaller as they grow outward.

3 Hone your thoughts to one word per branch (the biggest challenge and the biggest benefit).

4 Think about making symbols (squares, circles, triangles); you don't have to be a great artist.

5 Have your words, symbols or images sit on top of your branches.

6 Use colour to draw attention to different parts of your map.

By following these basic mind-mapping principles, you can get clarity on what a better memory can give you in the real world and what success looks like for you. This visual map will help you become aware of things you will need to learn, the challenges you may face and the specific actions you should take. You may even be surprised at some of the goals that appear, of which you were previously unaware.

The act of mind mapping or visual note taking naturally taps into our different types of intelligence:

- ▶ **Linguistic:** honing your thoughts to a single word and verbalizing to increase comprehension
- ▶ **Logical–mathematical:** creating structure, connections and patterns through branches, icons and symbols
- ▶ **Musical:** having a rhythm when you draw and summarize, playing music that inspires the tone of the map
- ▶ **Visual–spatial:** a mind map naturally lives in a three-dimensional, colourful and creative space
- ▶ **Body–kinaesthetic:** non-linear, acting out your maps, pointing to the various areas as you consolidate your thinking, to create a sense of what it is about
- ▶ **Emotional (intrapersonal, interpersonal):** triggering emotions as you travel through memories, imagine scenarios and create connections, making them engaging and memorable; sharing your map to spark curiosity, make others look for answers and guide problem solving

There are many ways to create your mind maps. You can use software (my preference is iMindMap, as it gives more visual control than others I have worked with), paper or whiteboard (one of my favourites, as you can easily remove and adapt if you change your mind). The following maps were created with iMindMap™ by ThinkBuzan.

Put a √ beside any or all of the areas you would like to grow in over the next 12 months:

Area of growth	Benefits
☐ 1 Physical wellbeing	Good health, fitness
☐ 2 Emotional health	Positive, motivated attitude, happiness
☐ 3 Relationships	Improved relations with family, friends, colleagues
☐ 4 Managing time	Current time maximized, more time freed up
☐ 5 Your passion/career/business	Better performance and results
☐ 6 Finances	Profits, savings
☐ 7 Level of contribution	Family, friends, everyone gains

Exercise 4

YOUR WORLD MAP: GOALS

In this activity you will create a mind map that reflects these seven key areas.

Think about the things you would like to achieve in these areas over the next 12 months.

Follow Jill as she maps out her goals in these seven key areas. Jill starts by creating a 'goals' branch off each of the key areas except 'emotional' (she will come back to this). As she thinks about the future, thoughts come to mind that reflect what success for her will look like. For example, her ideal physical body conjures up images of being fit and healthy, which in turn branches off specifics about her flexibility, weight, figure and even BMI.

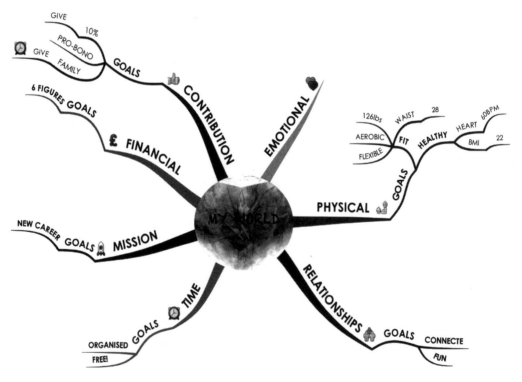

Jill's world map with goals, created using ThinkBuzan's iMindMap™
(www.thinkbuzan.com)

Now start to create your own world map in the space below, using Jill's example above as a guide and thinking about your own goals.

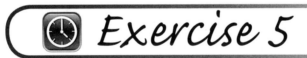

 YOUR WORLD MAP: CHALLENGES

Think now about what this future could be like, by mapping out the various obstacles that might slow you down, get in your way or completely block you. You may have thoughts like, 'I don't know enough about marketing', 'I'm not clever enough to make that kind of money' or 'I don't have enough time for my family and friends.'

Go back to your own map and add a branch called 'challenges' to each of the main topics (except for emotions) and note down what these challenges are for you.

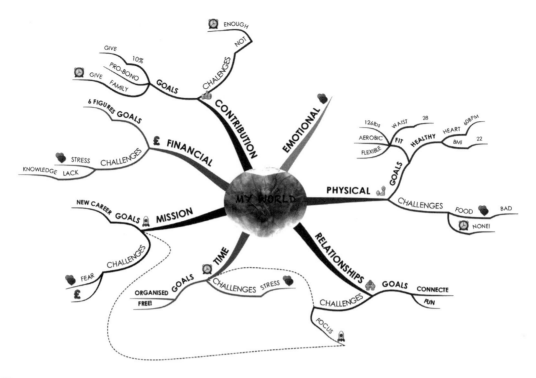

Jill's map with challenges added, created using ThinkBuzan's iMindMap™ (www.thinkbuzan.com)

Jill wants to manage stress and she can see that this is caused by her perceived lack of time and by financial pressures. She can also see that there is a pattern in terms of time, which comes up on the physical, time and contribution branches. She uses symbols to show these connections. Perhaps, if she learns to manage her time better, she will not only reduce her stress levels but also open up opportunities to get where she wants to be physically and make the kind of contributions she desires.

As in the example, notice whether any of your challenges 'connect' across branches. Use symbols or lines to show this on your own map.

By understanding how the challenges in your world connect, you will:

▶ **get clarity on what the problem is**
▶ **understand the impact of not taking action**
▶ **start to focus on potential options.**

Exercise 6

YOUR WORLD MAP: SKILLS, KNOWLEDGE AND FEELINGS

To overcome these challenges, you need to map out the skills and knowledge you will need to grow.

Focus now on the 'emotion' branch and reflect on the types of feelings you will need to experience and demonstrate to achieve your goals.

_____

_____

If you wanted to learn ballet, for example, you might start with the following:

▶ **Learn the relevant knowledge** (terminology like tondu, pirouette)
▶ **Perform the skills** (doing the tondu or pirouette technically correctly)
▶ **Experience the feelings** (confidence in your ability to perform in front of people)

Goals   From Jill's map overleaf we can see that she has ambitions to become fitter and healthier, be more connected in her relationships, become more organized so she can free up time to build a new career for herself and create an income of '6 figures'. She also wants to contribute more of her time and money to good causes.

Challenges   Stress, lack of time, liking bad food and a fear of failure are themes in Jill's challenges. These are slowing her down and stopping her from getting where she wants to be.

Skills and knowledge   Jill has identified areas of learning in terms of skills and knowledge that will help her overcome these challenges. She is also going to take more control of her emotions, feelings of stress and lack of time by taking up meditation and accelerating her ability to build her skills and knowledge through memory strategies. This map gives Jill a big-picture view of what her world could look like and the beginnings of a plan to achieve it.

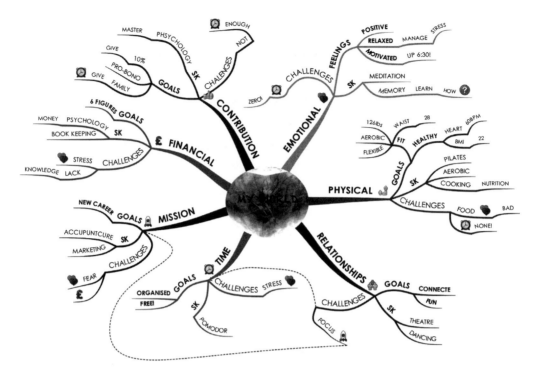

Jill's map with skills, knowledge and feelings added, created using ThinkBuzan's iMindMap™ (www. thinkbuzan.com)

→ Creating a user story

By making these connections and being clear on our goals, we can elaborate on the actions we need to take in order to move towards where we want to be. A good way to capture this is to use what is referred to as a user story. A user story has the following components:

1 AS A [how would you describe yourself?]

2 I WANT TO [take some positive action]

3 SO THAT I [can get beneficial results]

4 BY [target date].

In the example of Jill, her user story might be:

AS A successful businesswoman

I WANT TO learn…

- techniques to manage my stress levels
- how to better organize my time
- how to feel good about being healthy and fit
- how to move forward one specific area of business (accelerate acupuncture knowledge)
- how to overcome any fears about my business

… SO THAT I can achieve my goals of:

- helping people keep fit and healthy
- being more relaxed
- having a better work/life balance myself
- having financial success

BY June 2014.

Jill can choose how she wants to tackle each of the five points in her user story. This, combined with the mind map, will act as a guide to keep her on track.

Study your own mind map and either talk it through out loud or share it with a family member or a friend, taking in any relevant feedback and adding to your map. Mind maps are not static, and as your skills and knowledge grow so will your map. It will change as you move along your journey and perhaps even turn into something completely new.

→ Memory motivation

You now have some compelling reasons that will pull you forward towards your goals. However, in the same way that, for example, you may wake up in the morning and just not feel like going to the gym, those same types of feelings can present themselves when you think about spending 15 minutes improving your memory.

THE ROCKING CHAIR TECHNIQUE

The purpose of the rocking chair technique is to increase your motivation to achieve an excellent memory and realize that the benefits and value you get out will far outweigh the effort you put in.

You are about to be guided through two different timelines. Each timeline will have a different set of memories.

In the first timeline you will imagine a life where you didn't take any action to improve your memory. You are going to work to create as much pain associated with these memories as possible. This will create some urgency and reasons for making a positive change that will support you in your goals.

In the second timeline you will remember a life where you took decisive action, built your skills and knowledge and made a difference for yourself and others throughout your life. By helping your subconscious believe the second timeline as a reality, you will create some real motivation to drive you forward.

Imagine that you are 80 years old. You are sitting in a comfortable rocking chair. Picture where you are and whether any of your family members are with you. Start to notice your surroundings, and describe what you can see in as much detail as possible.

_____

_____

Describe what you can hear – noises, sounds and music.

_____

_____

→ How does all this make you feel?

As you sit here, start to look back on your life...

Timeline 1

In this timeline, remember the costs of not keeping your mind sharp and improving your memory. As you think back on your life, remember all the things you missed out on because you took no action. Think of how much time you wasted not moving forward on the things you hoped to learn and the things you hoped to achieve but never made an effort to do.

Spend a minute or so thinking about each of the following areas. Make it real and feel the feelings.

→ What did you miss out on in your own personal development?

_____

→ Did it affect any areas of your health? If so, what?

_____

→ What did you miss out on in your relationships?

_____

→ What business or career opportunities did you miss out on?

_____

→ Think about anything else you have missed out on: what could you have done differently?

_____

→ What are the regrets you now have about your life?

_____

Timeline 2

In this timeline, remember the benefits you gained from having an excellent memory. You have built your memory one day at a time, used it to grow your skills and knowledge, put it into practice to achieve results in your career and business, used it to help keep you sharp and healthy as you grew older, had more variety and fun in your life by being inspired to learn new things and share them with your family.

Sitting on your rocking chair looking back on your life, remember all the things you have done, shared, achieved and contributed.

→ In what personal development areas did you grow?

_____

→ What did you do that at one time you would have thought impossible?

_____

→ What have you done to remain healthy in your mind and body?

_____

→ In what way did you enhance your relationships with the people in your life because of your growth?

_____

→ What positive difference has this had on you, financially and in your career or business?

_____

→ How did you influence others because of your skills and knowledge?

_____

Spend some time enjoying these feelings and thinking about the positive impact you have made. Make it real and feel the feelings.

When you are ready, think about both these timelines and decide which one you would like to choose.

Now come back to the present. If you managed to make this real for yourself, you will have made a shift in your mind from thinking of an excellent memory as something you want to something that you *must* have.

Circle how many hours' effort this is worth to you in order to gain these kinds of benefits.

1   2   3   5   8   10+

Getting the right balance between effort and results can be tricky, especially when you are learning a new skill. This is something you can increase or decrease over time.

Summary

When you think of your memory, you should now have a picture of what the future could look like as you build your skills. You should also have a high level of motivation for taking action and following through.

Refer back to your persona and your mind map in this chapter as you go through the workbook, to remind yourself of the rewards and benefits you will receive as you travel to your destination.

What I have learned

→ What are my thoughts, feelings and insights on what I have read so far?

_____

_____

_____

Use the space below to summarize the actions to take as a result of reading this chapter.

_____

_____

_____

_____

Where to next?

In the next chapter you will discover how your memory works and learn ways to identify your strengths and weaknesses, so that you can see the areas where you need to improve. You will then benchmark your progress, to see how far you have come and how far you have to go to reach your goals.

2 Explore your memory

....

In this chapter you will learn:
- ▶ how your memory works
- ▶ ways to identify your strengths and weaknesses
- ▶ how to strengthen your working memory
- ▶ how to benchmark your current ability.

....

The aim of this chapter is to give you insights into how memory works, where your memory performs well and where you can improve. We will take a qualitative approach, meaning that you will gain insights about how you feel your memory is working and use this as a benchmark to measure your improvements as you progress.

The subject of memory is a vast one so, to simplify things and give some context, it is helpful to use some common terms to describe different types of memory.

Working memory (incorporating the idea of short-term memory) is your ability to focus attention, hold and manipulate information in your mind. You need this to evaluate and make decisions.

Long-term memory may be conscious (you are aware of doing something, i.e. you make an effort to remember) or non-conscious (you are unaware of doing something, i.e. you don't try to remember, but you do).

'Memory...is the diary that we all carry about with us.'

Oscar Wilde

The following table lists the different types of long-term memory, conscious and non-conscious, and what the different types mean.

Long-term memory type	Term	Meaning
Conscious	*Episodic*	Memory of your timeline of events and experiences throughout your life
	Semantic	Knowledge of facts
Non-conscious	*Procedural*	Getting 'how to' information into your body: tying your shoelaces, touch typing, riding a bike, playing a sport
	Priming	Raises attention: seeding your brain with upcoming terminology in a book that is then more familiar to you upon reading; buying a new gadget or dress and suddenly noticing other people with the same as you
	Conditioned	Habitual response to stimulus: seeing a police car flashing in your mirror, you respond without thinking – in a split second you check what else is around, slow down and let them pass, or perhaps panic! Whatever the response, it has been conditioned. Advertisers will prime you to become 'aware' and condition you for the response 'Buy me!'
	Emotional	A powerful motivator, primer and conditioner: it can be used to strengthen semantic and episodic memories but too much negative emotion can cause anxiety, stress and stop memory performing – you need to strike the right balance

Exercise 8

BECOMING AWARE

Come up with an example in your own life of each of the memory types described above (we will leave emotional memory for the moment) and fill in the following table.

Memory type	Your experience
Episodic	
Semantic	
Procedural	
Priming	
Conditioned	

Now that you have a sense of what each type of memory means to you in the real world, run through the next six exercises to get a deeper sense of how your memory performs and what you might do to support it.

 Exercise 9

YOUR EPISODIC MEMORY

Tick the areas where you think your episodic memory performs well:

☐ What happened yesterday

☐ Your last holiday

☐ Your past birthdays

☐ Your first date

☐ An early day at school

☐ Where you were during the opening of the Olympics 2012

☐ An experience after you left home

→ What positive experiences are memorable for you in your life? Note them below.

_____

_____

_____

_____

_____

_____

→ What was it about these experiences that made them memorable for you? Note them below.

_____

_____

_____

_____

_____

_____

Tick any of these boxes that you feel are relevant to those episodic memories:

☐ Vivid

☐ Time-tagged

☐ Emotional

☐ Good short-term

☐ Good long-term

Exercise 10

YOUR SEMANTIC MEMORY

Tick the areas where you think your semantic memory performs well:

☐ General knowledge

☐ Dates and birthdays

☐ Statistics

☐ Names of people

☐ Names of characters in a book

☐ Equations

☐ Phone, credit card and PIN numbers

☐ Facts in news and magazine stories

→ What information is memorable for you in your life? Note it below.

_____

_____

_____

_____

_____

_____

_____

→ What was it about this information that made it memorable for you? Note it below.

_____

_____

_____

Tick any of these boxes that you feel are relevant to those semantic memories:

☐ Vivid

☐ Valuable

☐ Emotional

☐ Good short-term

☐ Good long-term

 **Exercise 11**

YOUR PROCEDURAL MEMORY

Tick the areas where you think your procedural memory performs well:

☐ Learn dance steps

☐ Follow sequences

☐ Remember keyboard shortcuts

☐ Pick up controls on a computer game

☐ Play golf, cricket, tennis or badminton

☐ Do Pilates, yoga or martial arts

☐ Cook a recipe

☐ Ride a bike

☐ Play a musical instrument

➜ What 'how to' experiences are memorable for you in your life? Note them below.

_____

_____

_____

_____

_____

_____

➜ What was it about these experiences that made them easy to remember for you? Note them below.

_____

_____

_____

_____

_____

_____

Tick any of these boxes that you feel are relevant to those semantic memories:

☐ Reward

☐ Valuable

☐ Emotional

☐ Good short-term

☐ Good long-term

 *Exercise 12*

PRIMING YOUR BRAIN

Have you ever had the experience of buying a new item of clothing, gadget or car and suddenly you start noticing the same thing everywhere? Why do you think this is? Is it because everyone went out and bought the same thing at the same time? Unless you have been queuing outside the Apple store before the launch of a new iPad or iPhone, probably not. What's more likely is that because this item is now important to you or of interest to you, you start to notice similar things in your environment. You have primed your brain, so it is now programmed to look out for items that are similar. This taps into our instinctive nature to be curious and to look out for the things that are important to us.

To prime yourself:

▶ get curious, by asking questions that raise your interest (What could this book give me? What is interesting about this person? What am I going to hear in this workshop that's new?)
▶ guess what it could be
▶ be open to what comes back to you
▶ capture what comes back to you
▶ review what you have learned.

Create some priming questions for the following topics:

→ Names

1 _____

2 _____

3 _____

→ Books

1 _____

2 _____

3 _____

→ Problems

1 _____

2 _____

3 _____

→ Instructions

1 _____

2 _____

3 _____

→ Seminars

1 _____

2 _____

3 _____

→ Emails

1 _____

2 _____

3 _____

→ Magazines

1 _____

2 _____

3 _____

→ In what ways do you currently prime your brain? Note them below.

_____

_____

_____

_____

_____

_____

→ How might you use them to prime other areas of your life? Note your answers below.

_____

_____

_____

_____

_____

_____

_____

Tick any of these boxes that you feel are relevant to those priming experiences:

☐ Positive   ☐ Neutral

☐ Negative   ☐ Valuable

→ Conditioning our responses

About 15 years ago, I got into a two-seater plane with a pilot friend of mine. I had flown many times and never had a problem with it; in fact, I had always enjoyed it. My friend told me he was going to do a power dive and, although he explained exactly what would happen, when we went into the dive I felt an instant and irrational fear. Logically, I knew he had control of the plane, but my brain's amygdala – the specialist area for emotional matters – obviously thought otherwise and my internal alert system fired with a vengeance: 'fear'.

For a while after that incident, whenever I got on a plane I felt anxious in my gut, more so if it was a bumpy ride. The memory of this previous experience and the emotion associated with it always brought back a physiological reaction. I had been conditioned to respond in a certain way to flying.

I decided that I had to change this, so during the next bumpy flight I put on my headphones and played – loudly – the Kaiser Chiefs' album *Employment*. This produced an immediate change in state and I was able to zone into the rhythm of the plane bumping up and down. After about ten minutes of listening to the music, I was feeling stronger and actually started to enjoy the flight – waiting for the next bump. Memories of listening to this music, and the way it had made me feel before, came flooding back and it allowed me to condition myself to have a different response, one of strength and fun as opposed to feelings of fear.

YOUR CONDITIONED RESPONSES

Here you will explore your own conditioned responses to stimuli.

Choose one memory that you currently associate with:	What could you do to improve your current association with each area (even if it is positive)?
Learning:	
Studying:	
Reading:	
Exams:	
Career:	
Relationships:	

Money:	
Health:	

What effect would living with these new memories/associations have on your decisions? Make some notes below.

_____

_____

_____

_____

_____

Tick any of these boxes that you feel are relevant to those conditioned responses:

☐ Pleasure   ☐ Pain   ☐ Emotion

→ Emotions and memories

Personalizing our memories can make them more emotional and more powerful. As with the conditioned response example, the episodic memories that tend to stand out are the ones that make you feel different emotions.

You can make semantic information more memorable by creating an emotional story: something funny, exciting or scary. How primed and motivated might you be to learn, if you treat yourself with something that makes you feel great, once you find all the keywords in one book that would help you pass an exam? If you have ever danced or practised a martial art, perhaps you remember the emotion and feelings you had in your body that helped make it memorable.

YOUR EMOTIONAL MEMORY

Take the experiences you wrote about for Exercise 8 and capture below how you could involve your emotions to strengthen the memory of each of them.

Memory type	Your experience with emotion
Episodic	
Semantic	
Procedural	
Priming	
Conditioned	

→ Managing the executive

Visualization

Imagine this situation in as much detail as possible:

You are on a ship (the first thing that comes to mind; it could be the starship *Enterprise*). You are the captain. To your left and right are speakers (playing some cool music on a loop; hear the music). Above you is a 3D futuristic screen; you can create any image on this and bring it to life. Below you on your captain's chair is a control panel to access your captain's log, every experience you have ever had. On this control panel you can edit images from your screen and sounds from your speakers to create unique new episodes.

▶ What is directly to the left and right of you?

▶ What is directly above you?

▶ What is directly below you?

▶ Who are you?

The situation in the visualization represents the various components of Baddeley's model of working memory (first proposed in 1974). It sees the various elements as follows.

▶ **The captain is the central executive.**

The executive has the questions and directs operations. His executive board looks for the answers. This central idea acts as a conceptual placeholder to serve as a reminder of what remains to be explained.

▶ **The speakers are the phonological loop.**

The storage of verbal information, along with rehearsal mechanisms (saying something to yourself over and over again – 693, 693, 693), is important for short-term memory.

'Working memory – the term widely used by psychologists to refer to the set of cognitive processes involved in the temporary storage and manipulation of information.'

John H. Byrnes, 2009

▶ **The 3D screen is a visuospatial sketchpad.**

This stores visual and spatial information; creating visual images is important in emotional memory.

▶ **The control panel is the episodic buffer.**

This is the passive store that temporarily holds information from the phonological loop, visuospatial sketchpad and long-term memory. It binds these into episodes and is linked to the executive.

If you think of working memory in this way, you can imagine yourself as the executive asking questions and directing your board. Perhaps you want to imagine yourself as the captain of the USS *Enterprise*, bringing together all these systems when you want something to be memorable and transferred to your long-term memory.

Rather than just saying something over and over to get it into your head, you also get the visuospatial sketchpad involved. Think about what it looks like, how you can connect the sound with an image, what you already know about it from long-term memory, and what it means. How might you bind this information into a bigger chunk that is easier to remember and has meaning?

You might do this to remember a phone number. For example, take the number 5710062213:

1 First, chunk it up and use the phonological loop to keep it in your short-term memory: 571 – 006 – 2213.

2 Next, incorporate the visuospatial sketchpad and create an episode that you can transfer into long-term memory.

3 What does 571 remind you of? Heinz baked beans are the number 57 so have 1 big tin, 006 is 007's brother, 22 is two little ducks and 13 is unlucky for some.

4 You say 571 while looking at the tin of baked beans, say 006 as you see James Bond's brother eating the beans and say 2213 as two little ducks sitting on his shoulder do their business on his bright white jacket; he's obviously the unlucky brother.

5 Baked beans 1 tin, eaten by 006, with 2 ducks – as you see the image, you repeat 571 – 006 – 2213.

6 Now punch this number into your phone about five times. See how long it stays in your memory. Try it again tomorrow.

Although it takes some effort to combine all the systems, the outcome is a number that is now much more memorable than before.

Exercise 15

YOUR WORKING MEMORY

This performance task is a form of memory testing called N-Back training. Give yourself no more than ten minutes for this exercise to see how many aspects of working memory you can use to help you complete a task.

Decode the following words mentally. Work out the words by looking at a letter and counting two letters forward, i.e. A becomes C, Y becomes A, and R becomes T. In this way, AYR would be the word CAT.

You can choose to try this either with or without the alphabet below as a reference:

A B C D E F G H I J K L M N O P Q R S T U V W X Y Z

Write down the words in the spaces below. The first one is done for you. Start the clock when you are ready.

Coded word	Decoded
YRRCLRGML	*ATTENTION*
AMLBGRGMLCB	
CNGQMBGA	
QCKYLRGA	
NPMACBSPYJ	
NPGKGLE	

In terms of working memory, tick the areas in which you performed well:

☐ Attention (your ability to focus)

☐ Capacity (how much you can hold at any one time)

☐ Manipulation of data (your ability to manipulate the information in your mind)

N-Back training

There is some interesting preliminary research around N-Back training detailing increased intelligence. While it is yet to be confirmed, many people who go through a course of N-Back training claim a large improvement in attention and ability to focus, and that they feel sharper.

The dual N-Back task is more difficult because participants must keep both the visual string and the auditory string active in their working memory, while making decisions about each presentation. Try this task for yourself at www.achieve-with.me/memoryworkbook

→ Memory talk

Now you have some reference for the various memory types, think about the way you talk to yourself about your memory. You may often say things like:

▶ 'I'm good with faces but rubbish with names.'

▶ 'I'm good with numbers but no good with facts.'

▶ 'My memory is really bad.'

▶ 'I'm always forgetting things.'

▶ 'I can't remember his name!'

or you may say things like:

▶ 'It will come back to me.'

▶ 'Now, what was her name?'

▶ 'I know it's in there somewhere, what is it?'

Have you ever found that, when you ask the latter type of question, eventually – either soon after, or an hour or days or weeks later – the name, fact or detail comes flooding back? Perhaps you remember a time when you met someone on the street whom you hadn't seen in years, desperately tried to recall their name but were too embarrassed to ask, and then a week later it popped back into your head – Jamie!

 *Exercise 16*

SUPPORTING YOUR MEMORY

This exercise asks you to think about how you treat your memory, both when it performs poorly and when it performs well.

Think of a time when your memory has performed poorly. Describe the scenario below, including what you were thinking, feeling or saying to yourself. Write down whether you scolded or encouraged it.

_____

_____

_____

Now think of a time when your memory performed well. Where were you? What was happening? What were you thinking, feeling or saying to yourself? Again, include how you treated your memory. Did you take it for granted or did you congratulate and reward it? Describe the scenario below.

If you were to imagine your memory as a best friend, niece, nephew, son or daughter, what could you do to treat them in a way that would be more supportive and encouraging and get better results?

→ Create a list of actions below:

1 _____

2 _____

3 _____

→ Measure for measure

Now that you have a big-picture understanding of your memory, think about where you are and where you would like to be.

Exercise 17

BENCHMARKING YOUR PROGRESS

This is your own qualitative measure. You are going to benchmark where you believe you are at the moment and how far you have to go to get to your ideal goals.

1 For each of the following scales, decide what a 10 would mean for you. Write it in the box below the scale.

2 Decide what a 1 would be, and write it in the box.

3 Mark where you would rate your current memory abilities on the scale.

4 Imagine that you had the type of memory that would allow you to learn with ease the things you wanted to learn, to consume knowledge, new skills and feel confident that you could perform at your best. Think about what number you would love it to be and add this to the scales below.

→ Episodic memory

1 _____ 10

→ Semantic memory

1 _____ 10

→ Procedural memory

1 _____ 10

┌───┐
│   │
│   │
│   │
└───┘

→ Priming

1 _____ 10

┌───┐
│   │
│   │
│   │
└───┘

→ Conditioned response

1 _____ 10

┌───┐
│   │
│   │
│   │
└───┘

Summary

You should now have an understanding of how your memory works, where your strengths and weaknesses are and some ideas about how you can naturally improve your performance.

When you have got to the end of the book, come back to this chapter and do the benchmark activity again. Compare where you are when you finish with where you are now and note what insights you have gained.

What I have learned

→ What are my thoughts, feelings and insights on what I have read so far?

_____

_____

_____

Use the space below to summarize the actions to take as a result of reading this chapter.

_____

_____

_____

_____

Where to next?

In the next chapter you will enter the world of creative memorization, acquiring strategies to learn things more quickly, retain knowledge for longer and put what you know into practice.

3 Creative memorization

....

In this chapter you will learn:
- ▶ how creative memorization works
- ▶ how to make meaning from metaphor
- ▶ some effective memory-strengthening strategies.

....

Take a moment and think about what memory and learning mean to you. What comes to mind? Do you think about them in the past, present or future?

From my experience of asking this question of a variety of people over the years, it seems to me that memory tends to be more associated with the past, the experiences we've had, the things we know, the skills we have acquired, and encoding, storing and retrieving that information. Learning, on the other hand, tends to be more associated with the present and future, knowledge you have yet to consume, skills you could put into practice, events yet to happen. Creative memorization lives in both these worlds.

> 'The true sign of intelligence is not knowledge but imagination.'
>
> Albert Einstein

→ The art of memory

At the heart of creative memorization lies the 'art of memory' (classic mnemonic techniques and strategies). I view creative memorization through a slightly different lens, perhaps a wide-angle or panoramic lens that opens up the scope of possibilities. The idea behind this is that creative memorization isn't just about remembering. It is about creation, understanding and recall, and it forms the basis of our beliefs, the references to which we associate meaning and emotion.

To truly learn, you have to create; with creation and use comes understanding. If there is no memory, there can be no learning. Creative memorization binds these concepts and therefore its application offers us the opportunity to venture outside what might normally be considered the art of memory.

If you master your ability to create memories (past or future), you master your ability to motivate, understand, grow and achieve your goals. Olympic athletes understand this concept as they visualize outcomes of their events, creating memories that have not yet happened, wiring their brains to perform at an optimum level.

Likewise, creative memorization is not a passive form of remembering but a way of thinking that is results-focused and draws on each of your memory types (episodic, semantic, procedural, emotional, priming, conditioned response), looking for creative ways to make anything more memorable so that it can be understood and used. It enables your working memory to manipulate large chunks of information, increasing your ability to analyse, solve problems and form solutions.

Examples of such information that are useful to memorize include:

▶ Names of colleagues or clients

▶ Key topics for an interview

▶ Notes for an exam

▶ Cues for presentations

▶ Speeches in a script

▶ Knowledge in books

▶ Sequences in a dance routine

▶ Designing a metaphor to improve sports performance

How it works

Creative memorization is a strategy with four stages:

1 Memorize through creation

2 Remember through re-creation

3 Experiment through action

4 Grow through results

Exercise 18

THE 100 BILLION

Follow these simple steps to put creative memorization into practice.

▶ Get yourself relaxed.

▶ Think about what something means to you or reminds you of.

▶ Use your imagination and association around the meaningful memory to create a visual, auditory, kinaesthetic, olfactory, gustatory, emotional experience, which has meaning and is memorable.

As an example, try this:

Remember that there are 100 billion brain cells in the brain.

What does this mean to you or remind you of? Perhaps you know that it is the equivalent to Google's 100 billion web searches a month or the number of trees in the rainforest or the estimated number of planets in our galaxy.

How could you use your imagination and association to create a memorable experience? Write your thoughts here.

_____

_____

_____

_____

_____

_____

You might have written something like the following:

'There is a brain in space the size of a planet, which is searching on Google for trees in the rainforest, as he doesn't have any of his own.'

As you imagine this scene, you would involve your auditory sense and say aloud, 'There are 100 billion neurons in the brain, 100 billion planets in our galaxy, 100 billion searches on Google every month and 100 billion trees in the rainforest.'

If you are more kinaesthetic, you might imagine you are the brain in space!

The above example does two things:

▶ It makes the information memorable.
▶ It gives you real-world context by comparing the brain with the galaxy, with Google and with the rainforest, creating understanding.

You will notice that it doesn't matter that this is completely unrealistic. You would never have a brain the size of a planet looking for trees on Google just because he doesn't have any of his own. However, by creating meaning in the association, the scene becomes more memorable.

→ Flow

> *'Flow is a state in which an individual is completely immersed in an activity without reflective self-consciousness but with a deep sense of control.'*
>
> Stefan Engeser, 2012

Athletes often refer to being 'in the zone' when they experience flow. The great actor–director Stanislavsky talked about flow as 'the artistic condition that frees the body of tension and energizes the creative faculties'.

Have you ever been in a situation when you were talking in front of a group of people and you had a momentary blank? What happened next? Were you like a rabbit in the headlights? The harder you tried to remember what to say the more anxious you became, until the mental block just shut you down. You may have experienced this in an exam situation, a driving test or something similar.

As far as memory is concerned, when this state happens we become unresourceful. Anxiety and stress can shut down activity in the prefrontal cortex, where your higher thinking happens. Our amygdala may then take over, and we resort to our fight-or-flight instinct. This is when we hear our inner voice saying, 'Get me off this stage!' or 'Get me out of this exam!'

What is the difference between someone in the above state and a person who is 'in the zone'? The person in the latter state seems completely confident and present in the moment. This is a person who seems to know the 'right things to say', makes you feel they 'know what they're doing' and looks relaxed and energized. They have achieved flow.

We have all experienced this, at times when things were just happening for us and where everything we did felt right:

▶ The right words came to mind.

▶ We moved in a natural and energetic way.

▶ We felt confident and present in the moment.

This may have happened to you when you were giving a talk, acting, playing a sport, taking an exam, teaching, making a sales pitch or teaching your children something. When you were in this state, your body would have moved in specific ways, using certain gestures, and you might have used specific language and a particular tone of voice; you will also have had a set of positive feelings connected with this experience.

This is the state of flow: it describes the feeling you have when you are completely present and things just happen for you. This is the state of relaxation and energy you are looking for in creative memorization.

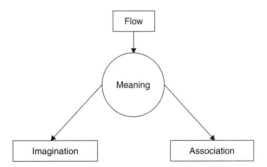

The state of 'flow' and creative memorization

Exercise 19

CREATING FLOW

Being able to get into a state of flow is the first part of creative memorization. When you are in this state, you become less self-conscious, time can fly by and you feel driven to move forward.

Think about a time when you were in a state of flow. It's most likely a time when you had a clear purpose, you felt confident and immersed, you had a feeling that you could adapt to the situation, and you had a lightning focus and sense of certainty.

Re-create a memory from the past that closely mirrors this feeling. If nothing comes to you immediately, remember a time when you were doing something you love. Make it real, include all your senses and describe it in as much detail as possible.

→ What is happening in your body?

_____

_____

→ What type of words are you using?

_____

_____

→ What type of pictures do you see in your mind?

_____

_____

→ What does it mean to you when you are in this state?

_____

_____

→ When you think about this state of flow, where is this feeling in your body, what might it look like, what does it feel like, what could it sound like?

_____

_____

Focus in on the area of your body where this feeling is at its most intense and stay with it for a moment.

Now give this feeling of flow an action that will bring it back to you at any time. Perhaps you bring your hands together touching the tips of your fingers and say the word 'flow'. If the state is intense and real enough, this will start to create a conditioned response, so whenever you touch the tips of your fingers together in this way and say 'flow', it brings you into this state.

Repeat this until the feeling is at a 9 or 10.

→ What would happen if you could instantly create this state at will?

_____

_____

Take a break and, when you are ready, test it out.

Being able to get into this state is just the first part of creative memorization. The second part is being able to use your creativity in such a way that you can give anything more meaning and make it more memorable. In order to do this, you need to tap into a way of thinking that is instinctively natural to all of us; we may have just buried the skill deep within ourselves. This creative skill is our ability imaginatively to associate things together.

→ Looking for meaning

Powerful ways of making something meaningful and memorable or getting information into your body are analogies, metaphors and similes. Let us look at the definitions of these.

- **A metaphor** is a symbol or phrase that represents something else: 'Something is something.' An example is 'You are a couch potato.'
- **A simile** equates two different things: 'Something is like something or as a something.' 'Life is like a box of chocolates'; 'He's as cunning as a fox.'
- **An analogy** compares similarities in relationships: 'Dogs are to puppies as cats are to kittens.' What is being compared are the 'relationships' between the two things (i.e. dogs/puppies and cats/kittens).

Years ago I played Gus, a character in Pinter's play *The Dumb Waiter*. To get me started I thought about his physicality. A visual metaphor came to mind: Gus is a friendly gorilla. With one thought, I had taken a mass of information into my body.

Exercise 20

CREATING METAPHORS

The purpose of using metaphors is to make something memorable and add meaning to it. The metaphors you create don't need to be clever.

Read the combinations of words in the table below and write down your own metaphors. The first example has been done for you.

Words	Direct connection	Metaphor	Expand metaphor
The brain and Google	*You don't need to think too hard with your brain to use Google.*	*Your brain is the ultimate Google.*	*Your brain is the ultimate Google: you only have to ask to get an answer, although it may require several searches to get what you want.*
Learning and salmon			
Belief and table			
Intelligence and space			
Memory and water			
Facebook and pizza			

Making it stick

In creative memorization, imagination and association are the mental glue that makes things stick.

Imagination represents our ability to bring to life experiences using our senses and emotion.

Association is our ability to question, analyse and make connections.

Exercise 21

TEST YOUR MEMORIZATION SKILLS

This exercise brings together the skills you have learned in the previous two exercises. Within the following story are 15 random items. Rather than trying to remember these items just as they are, you will use your imagination and associative skills to create this story in your mind, making it as vivid as possible so that you will remember the items more easily.

This doesn't necessarily mean that you have to 'see' everything in 3D (although you can learn this skill too). If you are auditorily inclined, you may want to read the story out loud and let the images come to mind; if you are more kinaesthetic, you may prefer to imagine that you are in the story, directing what happens next.

You may find that halfway through you feel compelled to go back to the beginning of the story, but avoid this distraction and keep going. Imagine each connection as clearly as you can, incorporating as many of your senses as possible. This in turn may spark off some emotion.

Imagine the following story:

Big Ben is wearing **a fur coat** and bouncing up and down on a **springboard.** He dives into a large **pot of honey**, and out of the honey comes a **dinosaur** wearing a **red baseball cap** and swinging a **baseball bat**. It starts smashing up a **Ferrari** with the baseball bat. Driving the Ferrari is **Tom Cruise**, who is smoking a **huge cigar**. Tom looks over to his right and stubs out the cigar on the head of a **bald man**. The bald man is eating a big sticky **Mars bar**, and wrapped around the Mars bar is **a slimy snake**, playing the **drums** and drinking a bottle of **Budweiser**.

Run through the story twice more, increasing your pace each time.

Now cover over the story and write down below the 15 items that were shown in bold.

1	6	11
2	7	12
3	8	13
4	9	14
5	10	15

You will probably have remembered more than ten items. If not, you simply need to create stronger associations.

→ Reference stories

Often, all you have to do with creative memorization is get into a good state, look for some meaning, turn key information into sensory images and associate those together. However, when you have more complex information or words that don't immediately spark off an image, there is another way to use creative memorization, which involves using sets of images called 'reference stories'.

For example, how might you remember the following word and its definition?

Confabulate: engage in conversation

You already have the meaning, but in order to turn this into a memorable image or set of images you may choose to use:

▶ natural images: two people engaged in fabulous conversation

▶ sound images: two coins looking fabulous engaged in conversation

The first images are naturally sparked off, while the second set of images uses the word 'coins' as it sounds like the first part of the word: coin-fabulate. It therefore acts as a trigger image for the real word. For both examples, it is important that you hear and speak the words aloud as you see the images.

Using natural or sound images is a personal thing. Associations offered by someone else will never be as good as associations you come up with yourself. However, as you begin to condition your brain to think in this way, it's good to have plenty of examples to give you a kick-start. These sets of images are 'reference stories' because they refer to the real information. Here is an example of how to remember that the Russian for cow is *karova*.

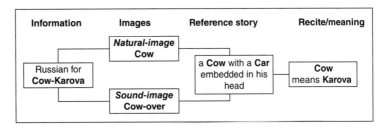

Encoding a reference story

With repetition and use, the reference story is not needed (even though it will be there as a safety net if it's a strong association), as you simply know that *karova* means cow.

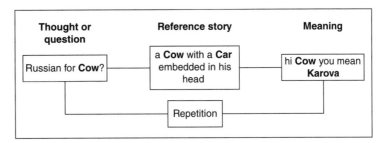

Decoding a reference story

CREATING REFERENCE STORIES

Create some short reference stories to remember this list of inventions and their inventors. The first four examples have been done for you. By searching Wikipedia, you can use real people rather than sound or natural images as here.

Inventions and inventors	Reference stories
Electric battery – Alessandro Volta	*Alice* in wonderland sitting in the *sand* with a high -*volt*age *battery*
Photography – Fox Talbot and Daguerre	A *Fox* down the *Talbot* pub waving a *dagger* and being *photographed*
Miners' lamp – Humphry Davy	A *miners' lamp* being worn by *Humpty Davy*
Electromagnet – William Sturgeon	*William* loved going fishing for *sturgeon* with his *electromagnet*
Waterproof clothes – Charles Macintosh	
Microphone – Charles Wheatstone	
Lawnmower – Edwin Budding	
Refrigeration – Jacob Perkins	
Revolver – Samuel Colt	
Postage stamp – Rowland Hill	
Vacuum cleaner – Hubert Booth	
Traffic lights – J. P. Knight	

Now cover up your reference stories and test your knowledge.

1 Who invented the microphone?

a Charles Wheatstone

b J. P. Knight

c Humphry Davy

2 What did William Sturgeon invent?

a Refrigeration

b Revolver

c Electromagnet

3 What did Alessandro Volta invent?

a Electric battery

b Traffic lights

c Vacuum cleaner

4 Who invented photography?

a Hubert Booth and Fox Talbot

b Fox Talbot and Daguerre

c Daguerre and Samuel Colt

5 What did Edwin Budding invent?

a Postage stamp

b Lawnmower

c Electric battery

6 Who invented waterproof clothes?

a J. P. Knight

b Charles Macintosh

c Charles Wheatstone

7 Who invented the postage stamp?

a Rowland Hill

b Jacob Perkins

c Fox Talbot and Daguerre

8 What did J. P. Knight invent?

a Revolver

b Traffic lights

c Microphone

9 Who invented the miner's lamp?

a Charles Wheatstone

b Humphry Davy

c Hubert Booth

10 Who invented refrigeration?

a Jacob Perkins

b J. P. Knight

c Alessandro Volta

Throughout the workbook, where you are asked to create reference stories, you can choose whether you want to write them down or do them in your head. Both methods are equally valid, but with practice the latter is the goal. This is also a great workout for your working memory.

→ Strengthening your images

At times, your images and associations may not feel as vivid or as strong as they could be. The following two strategies give some options for locking your creations in your mind over long periods of time.

DIALLING UP

Rather than trying to 'force' your images and associations to be bigger and brighter, incorporating more senses and emotion, it can be more effective to use a visual metaphor and let your subconscious do the work.

▶ Stand up and imagine that right out in front of you is a dial.

▶ Touch this dial and imagine it in as much detail as possible. Use all of your senses.

▶ Visualize the numbers 1 to 10 around it, or you may prefer to use colours blue through to bright yellow or some other combination that looks and feels right to you.

▶ You can now use this tool to dial up or down your memories and creations.

Try this: Remember the Big Ben story in Exercise 21.

▶ Go to the point in the story where the dinosaur is coming out of the honey.

▶ Look at your dial and decide (if you are using numbers) what number you are currently at (1 is virtually nothing and 10 is the most vivid experience you could imagine).

▶ Now turn the dial on your memory up a couple of notches and notice what happens (this is different for everyone).

▶ Now turn it down to a 2 on your dial and notice what happens.

▶ Play with this for a few minutes, noticing the differences as you dial up and down your memories.

▶ Turn your dial up to an 8, 9 or 10 and run through the whole Big Ben story at this level.

Capture your experience in the space below.

Using this visual metaphor means you don't have to think about all the separate senses and emotions: your subconscious will do the work for you. Everyone's experience is different with this technique, so you may find you zoom in, incorporate more colour, objects may grow arms and legs and sing or dance, feelings can become stronger, or everything may come to life.

As your experience with creative memorization grows and you create stronger images, you can adapt your scale, so that what was once your 10 may become your 7, so you have somewhere to go.

 *Exercise 24*

REMOTE CONTROL

Here is another visual metaphor that is excellent at speeding up your ability to recall your images and transfer what you have memorized into your long-term memory.

- ▶ Imagine you are holding a memory remote control.
- ▶ As you study it, you notice that there are play, fast-forward and rewind buttons, and you may also notice other details.

Try this: Again, remember the Big Ben story.

- ▶ Bring up Big Ben and press play on your remote control.
- ▶ When you get to the end, press the rewind button.
- ▶ Once back at the beginning, press fast forward.
- ▶ Your remote has many speeds: fast forward and rewind your movie several times, going faster each time.

Capture your experience in the space below.

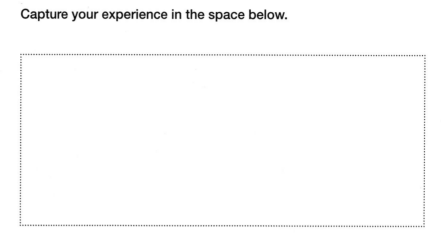

Once you have run the movie technique, you should find that your ability to recall information at speed increases, as well as the strength of your memories.

→ Affective memory

Do you have trouble visualizing? When I use the term visualize, I am talking about your ability to see images, hear sounds, create emotion and feelings.

Stanislavsky, the great Russian actor and director, had a technique called affective memory, which actors used to produce emotional states through their senses. It was broken down into 'sense memory' and 'emotional recall'. By practising these techniques, your ability to visualize will rapidly evolve.

 **Exercise 25**

 USING SENSE MEMORY

Try this technique to amplify your sensory experiences.

▶ Find an object, perhaps a toy car or something similar. Study it, using each of your senses in turn (sight, sound, smell, touch and taste).

▶ Do this for at least three minutes.

▶ Close your eyes and recreate it in your mind's eye.

- Repeat the opening and studying and then closing your eyes, recreating it several times.
- Move the object away from you and recreate it as if it were there in front of you (you don't need to remember every detail; your focus should be getting your senses engaged).
- Describe it out loud in as much detail as possible, imagining that you can see it there and pick it up. How heavy is it? What does it feel like – rough or smooth? Does it smell of anything? If you were to lick it, what would it taste like? Build up a concrete image using each of your senses, continuing to ask yourself questions about its look, sound, touch, smell and taste.

Practise this activity for up to ten minutes a day over the next three weeks to improve your visualization skills. You can choose different objects, large and small.

 Exercise 26

USING EMOTIONAL RECALL

Use the same object as in the previous activity. This time you are going to use it to create emotion and feeling. This works by taking the object into a past or future memory, which can be real or make-believe as long as it 'feels real'. Let's imagine you have a toy car:

- Hold the toy car in your hand and study it in as much detail as you did in the sense memory exercise above.
- Bring this car with you far into the future. Imagine you are in a rundown old bedsit with ragged curtains and dim lighting. You find yourself staring at this small toy car, thinking about memories of the past.
- Come back to the present and imagine that you are now standing on a stage, holding this car in the air and smiling. As you look out into the audience, you see hundreds of expectant faces.
- What emotions did you start to feel for each of these experiences and what were the differences?

Capture your experience in the space below.

```
┌─────────────────────────────────────────────────────┐
│                                                       │
│                                                       │
│                                                       │
│                                                       │
│                                                       │
│                                                       │
│                                                       │
│                                                       │
│                                                       │
└─────────────────────────────────────────────────────┘
```

Try the same thing again, taking the toy car into these scenes:

→ Lying on a beach sunning yourself, holding the car up in front of you

→ Standing at the edge of a tall building with the car gripped tightly in your left hand

→ Playing with a child and hearing a creaking noise from upstairs

By focusing on the object while putting yourself inside a scenario, not only does the object become more memorable but, once you have accessed the emotion you are looking to create, the object can act as a trigger for that emotion. This is a powerful tool used by actors, and it is also useful when it comes to bringing your memories alive.

→ Internal vs external

Think about the last time you ate a piece of fruit. Picture it in your mind. Now imagine that that piece of fruit is in front of you right now. What difference do you notice, in the context of how it feels?

It is likely that when you remembered the piece of fruit there was a feeling that it was more 'internal', maybe 'in the past', and that when you imagined the piece of fruit in front of you it was more 'external' and 'right now'. Differentiating between these experiences and knowing when to use one over the other can be very valuable.

Let's say you were giving a presentation to a group of people and you had memorized a set of visual cues; think of this as having a PowerPoint in your mind. Would you have preferred this mental PowerPoint to be somewhere inside your head or right out in front of you, in the room? Most likely, it is the latter. The benefit of this is that you can remain in the present, the 'now', as opposed to looking internally and drawing out what comes next.

If you have ever seen *Minority Report* or *The Avengers,* you will remember scenes in the films where a character brings up a 3D screen, which they can interact with. This is the idea I will use when I talk about projecting externally. We will call this the iMind.

USING YOUR IMIND

Use your iMind to project the Big Ben story externally:

▶ Stand up as if you were about to give a presentation (you could imagine that each image in the Big Ben story represented a topic).

▶ Run through the Big Ben story, projecting it right out in front of you.

▶ As you project it you can also manipulate the images, make them bigger, smaller and move them around.

▶ Get physical: you can point at items, grab them, throw them out in front, behind, above or below you.

▶ Now tell the full story of Big Ben out loud in your own words, using the images in the room as a set of visual cues.

Capture your experience in the space below.

This strategy may take some getting used to, but it is highly beneficial in any situation where you need to be absolutely present, such as when making a presentation or during meetings and interviews.

Summary

In this chapter you have begun building your memory skills, experiencing the ideal state of flow, understanding the power of metaphor, and using your creative ability to glue and strengthen information in your mind. Now you can start to ask yourself the question, 'Where can I start putting this way of thinking into practice?' and let your ultimate Google machine do the searching for you.

What I have learned

→ What are my thoughts, feelings and insights on what I have read so far?

_____

_____

_____

Use the space below to summarize the actions to take as a result of reading this chapter.

_____

_____

_____

_____

Where to next?

In the next chapter we will be looking at some key memory strategies from 'the art of memory'. These strategies will offer you the ability to acquire large amounts of knowledge quickly and easily.

4 Memory strategies

- -

In this chapter you will learn:

▶ how to put the chain method into practice
▶ how to establish memory networks – your mental filing systems
▶ strategies to apply in your own world.

- -

If you have any experience with memory techniques or mnemonics, you may have heard of strategies such as the chain method, link systems, the Roman room method, number shape and number rhyme systems, peg systems, the body system, the memory palace, the journey system and the method of loci. All of these and others serve one of two different purposes: they either let you take sequences of images and connect them together to form a type of mental chain (as with the Big Ben story in the previous chapter) or they allow you to use a predefined sequence of items and attach new information to those items. For example, you could imagine using your feet, knees, thighs, behind, waist, chest, neck, face and hair as a sequence you know well. You could then attach images to this mental filing system.

> 'Memory is the mother of all wisdom.'
>
> Aeschylus

The chain method and the method of loci are deceptively simple and, because of this, their true value can be overlooked. Many people who have tried to develop memory strategies get no further than memorizing simple shopping lists or other short data sets. While this is an excellent place to start, to truly realize the benefits of these strategies you need to dive in and become practised at using them, and then you can look for various ways to apply them in your life.

→ The chain method

When you first start to use the chain method, it is generally best not to use any real information, because in the beginning it can be a distraction to the process itself. Instead, focus on using a list of random objects or items, as mentioned previously. This way, you will gain a deeper and quicker understanding of the steps you need to take and what it feels like to remember a lot of information and retain it. The Big Ben story is an example of this: the images do not reference anything and the story is simply demonstrating that you have the ability to easily remember 15 items – in sequence, forwards and backwards – and retain your memory of them over a long period of time.

Before working on your chaining skills, you can use another technique called connecting the chain. It works by joining together the first and last item in a sequence. In the Big Ben story, the first item is Big Ben and the last is Budweiser, so you might imagine the snake passing the beer to Big Ben. This will connect the chain together, forming a stronger memory and allowing you to run the chain from any point forwards or backwards.

Here are seven tips for creating rapid, long-lasting chains:

1 Get into a flow state.

2 Look for meaning.

3 Create your images and associations.

4 Articulate the words aloud.

5 Connect the chain.

6 Dial up your memory.

7 Run your remote.

Be aware of potential blockers, such as:

▶ spending too much time on the initial 'pass'

▶ holding on too tight

▶ thinking about what's 'right' (there are no rules, just guidelines)

▶ creating too much complexity.

Exercise 28

CHAIN REACTION

This is a stamina game to help immerse you in the chain method. You will need a timer, and to give yourself five minutes to create a story from the words in each list. Test your memory after you complete all four lists. In the beginning, go for a rhythm that moves you along at a steady pace; don't overthink or try to create the perfect story.

Below the table you'll find examples for the first two lists if you need a kick-start, but it is much more effective if you can personalize them for yourself. The following four chains contain 20 items each.

Chain no.	Items	Your story
1	BOOK, CURTAIN, RING, LAMP, CAR, CHAIR, CHOCOLATE, CLOCK, KNIFE, PAINT, CARPET, GLASS, TREE, BRUSH, STATUE, PENCIL, COAL, PLANT, ROPE, GLOVE	
2	SUN, STINGRAY, BOOT, SHARK, KEY, MONKEY, WATER, RAT, DAM, SPIDER, RAIN, DUCK, CHICKEN, ROCKET, NET, SOLDIER, MAT, HORSE, MAP, ELEPHANT	
3	SYRUP, WILL, CLOUD, WHEELS, EARTH, FROST, CAVE, SEEDS, EXPLOSION, RUBY, WALLET, ISLAND, ARROW, LAMB, VOLCANO, FINGER, STICK, HOLE, KNIGHT, FEATHER	
4	TRAIN, SAND, SATURN, COWBOY, VORTEX, BUBBLES, ENTERPRISE, WEB, JAVELIN, DANCE, CRACKER, SONIC, MOUNTAIN, TRAINER, CABIN, DEVIL, SOUP, EMERALD, CAPE, BLADE	

Here are ideas for the first two examples:

▶ Imagine a gigantic **book** grabbing **curtains** that are hanging on a **ring**. The ring is thrown over a **lamp** that goes flying through a **car** window. Driving the car is a **chair** covered in **chocolate**, on top is a **clock** and you cut the clock in half with a **knife** covered in blue **paint**. The paint spills over your **carpet** made of **glass**. The glass grows into a **tree** that is covered in **brushes**. A brush falls off and hits a **statue** on the head; the statue picks up a **pencil** made of **coal** and ties up a **plant** with a **rope**. The rope is burning so it puts on a **glove**.

▶ Out of the **sun** flies a **stingray** that crashes into a large leather **boot**. The boot is eaten by a **shark** holding the magic **key**, the cheeky **monkey** steals the key and dives into the **water**, scaring a **rat** who escapes by running up a **dam,** only to be eaten by a gigantic **spider**. The spider is sad that no one likes him so he starts singin' and dancing in the **rain**. The **duck** and **chicken** that are watching find this so funny that they decide to fly off in their **rocket**. The rocket gets trapped in a **net** that is held by a **soldier** bouncing on a **mat**. The mat is eaten by a **horse**, which is reading a **map** trying to give directions to Edward the **Elephant**.

Now test your recall by covering the table above and listing the items below.

Chain no.	Items
1	
2	
3	
4	

CREATIVE CHAINS

The time limit for this exercise is ten minutes.

Using your knowledge of creative memorization, you are going to come up with an image to reference each of the words in the following four lists and create a set of mental chains. You are likely to need to use a combination of sound images and natural images.

Chain no.	Items
1	PREPARATION, AROUSAL, INTEREST, GOAL, BENEFITS, PHYSICAL, EMOTIONAL, SOCIAL, SUGGESTIONS, FEARS, BARRIERS, INVOLVEMENT
2	PRESENTATION, ENCOUNTER, COLLABORATE, OBSERVATION, BRAIN, BODY, INTERACTIVE, COLOURFUL, STYLE, PROJECT, DISCOVER, WORLD, PROBLEM
3	PRACTICE, INTEGRATE, PROCESSING, TRIAL, SIMULATION, GAME, ACTIVITY, ARTICULATE, DIALOGUE, TEACH, SKILLS
4	PERFORMANCE, PLAN, APPLICATION, REINFORCE, MATERIALS, COACHING, EVALUATE, PEERS, ORGANIZATION

Here's an idea for chain no. 1:

▶ Imagine **preparing** an appetizer that is **arousing** lots of **interest**, and as you throw it into a **goal** you are showered with hundreds of **benefits**. You grab a **dumbbell** with your right hand and your **heart** starts pounding out of your chest, all of your **friends** come over with a box of **suggestions**, but inside the box is a **fear** creature, which breaks out and jumps on top of a **barrier**, and everyone else decides to get **involved.**

Now test your recall by covering the table above and listing the items below.

Chain no.	Items
1	
2	
3	
4	

Make sure you have run all seven strategies for creating rapid, long-lasting chains:

1 Get into a flow state.

2 Look for meaning.

3 Create your images and associations.

4 Articulate the words aloud.

5 Connect the chain.

6 Dial up your memory.

7 Run your remote.

THE 125 TEST

You should now have memorized 125 words, and this exercise will check this.

▶ Recite all 125 items from the previous two exercises out loud, in sequence.

▶ Choose any two of the lists and bring them into your iMind, projecting them in front of you. Imagine you are giving a speech.

→ Using story cubes

A great way to practise the chain method is with a set of Rory's Story Cubes, available from www.storycubes.com

These cubes are dice with a different image on each face, and you can play many games with them that will expand your associative skills. With just one set there are over 10 million combinations. (Children love this game!)

To play, roll the dice and tell a story that connects the images together. For example:

'Once upon a time... there was a rusty fountain, home to thousands of bugs. One bug decided he had had enough, so he made a call on his mobile phone, ended up on the mystic tree and jumped on to the

Rory's story cubes

back of a star for a ride. After months of adventure he came upon a wand which teleported him to the top of a skyscraper in the city. He leaped off and landed outside the door of a chocolate house, and as he knocked on the door a big learner sign fell on his head. For the first time he wished he was back in his fountain.'

INCREASING YOUR RHYTHM

One of the challenges you may face is memorizing at high speed. In the beginning you may lose accuracy, especially if, when you think 'speed' or 'faster', it creates tension. If you find this happening to you, think of a metaphor or an idea that would allow you to increase your rhythm and still remain in a state of flow. Perhaps you flow down the river of knowledge? Or maybe you increase the rhythm of your thoughts?

Design your metaphor in the space below.

→ Your memory networks

At the beginning of this chapter, you read the story of how Simonides of Ceos demonstrated the method of loci. Also mentioned were other systems – such as peg systems, the body system, the memory palace and the journey system – which all offer a structured approach to storing and retrieving ideas, knowledge or skills – a mental filing system.

Peg systems are usually sequences of images like '1 bun, 2 shoe and 3 tree', etc., on which you 'hang' information. Methods of loci include systems like memory palace and the journey method, where you use separate locations within a room or locations along a journey. All of these memory networks consist of a set of memory files in which you can store knowledge. Think of it like this:

▶ Your **brain** is the **Internet** – it's vast.

▶ **Memory networks** are **websites** – you can create a lot!

▶ **Memory files** are **web pages** – so you can find what you're looking for.

▶ Your knowledge, ideas and skills are your **content**.

Your capacity for creating these memory networks is virtually unlimited. The following exercises will show you how.

Exercise 32

USING THE BODY SYSTEM

In this activity the body system is the memory network, the memory files are the different parts of your body and the items in it are your content. To make them stick, all you have to do is associate them. Here are some example associations, but ideally you should go ahead and create your own, writing them down in the fourth column.

Chain no.	Item	Association	Your association
1 Feet	Bomb	A bomb blowing up at your feet	
2 Knees	Balloons	Coloured balloons lifting your knees into the air	
3 Thighs	Leaf	A sticky leaf wrapped around your thighs	
4 Behind	Bee	A gigantic bumble bee stinging your behind	
5 Waist	Boar	A cuddly wild boar running around your waist	
6 Chest	Car	007's car revving on your chest	
7 Neck	Knight	A knight's armour worn around your neck	
8 Face	Oxygen	You are sucking a blue oxygen mask	
9 Hair	Toothpaste	Washing your hair with toothpaste	
10 Ceiling	Neon sign	Your name in neon lights on the ceiling	

Now test your recall by covering the associations above and listing the items below.

Chain no.	Item
1 Feet	
2 Knees	
3 Thighs	
4 Behind	
5 Waist	
6 Chest	
7 Neck	
8 Face	
9 Hair	
10 Ceiling	

 Exercise 33

 THE MEMORY PALACE

In this exercise your home is the memory network, the memory files are the objects in your rooms and the items are your content. We will number these files 11–30. The numbering isn't always important, but it will serve our purpose here.

To design your memory palace, choose four rooms in your home and from each room pick out just five items. It's recommended that you do this in a clockwise direction. If you were to enter your living room, look to your left and see a chair, that chair would be file no.11; if the next item was a window, that would be file no.12; if the next was a TV, that would be no.13; and so on.

By chunking your files into groups of five, you make it easy to remember the sequence.

▶ Write the names of your four rooms below.

▶ Choose and write down five objects from each room.

▶ Close your eyes and run each group of five objects forwards and backwards until the sequence feels strong.

Room 1:		Room 2:	
11		16	
12		17	
13		18	
14		19	
15		20	
Room 3:		Room 4:	
21		26	
22		27	
23		28	
24		29	
25		30	

▶ Now memorize the following 20 items by associating them to your files in order:

→ Salt, Magazine, Ale, Silly cone, Fozzie Bear Surfer, Swimming pool, Aga oven, Pots, Milk, Scanner, Tights, Van, Chrome wheels, Man kneeling, Iron, Cobbles, Coin, Policeman, Sink

▶ Recite all 30 items from this and the last exercise, starting with the item you associated to 'feet' all the way through to the last file in your memory palace. Do this now.

▶ Think about the images. What knowledge do you think you have consumed? Check through the following list and realize that you have just memorized the first 30 elements of the periodic table, along with their atomic numbers.

The body system and first five in the memory palace	The remaining 15 in the memory palace
1 Hydrogen bomb	16 Surfer for Sulphur
2 Helium balloon	17 Swimming pool for Chlorine
3 Leaves sounds like Li for Lithium	18 Aga oven for Argon
4 Bee for Beryllium	19 Pots for Potassium
5 Boar for Boron	20 Milk for Calcium
6 Car for Carbon	21 Scanner for Scandium
7 Knight for Nitrogen	22 Tights for Titanium
8 Oxygen	23 Van for Vanadium
9 Fluoride toothpaste for Fluorine	24 Chrome wheels for Chromium
10 Neon lights	25 Man on knees for Manganese
11 Salt for Sodium	26 Iron
12 Magazine for Magnesium	27 Cobbles for Cobalt
13 Ale for Aluminum	28 Coin for Nickel
14 Silly cone for Silicon	29 Policeman for Copper
15 Fozzie Bear for Phosphorous	30 Sink for Zinc

→ Journeys in your life

Here is an example of a brainstorm session with a client, where we started to scratch the surface of creating memory networks by probing episodic memory, the experiences a person has had throughout their life.

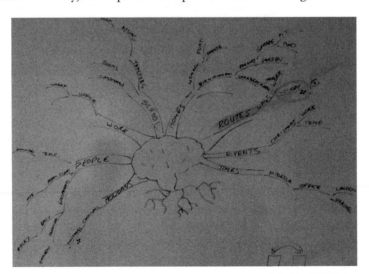

The first journey created was sparked off by the holiday branch of his mind map (circled). This transported him back to a place he went to when he was a child, and allowed him to create his first ten files (there were many more derived from just this one keyword):

1	Caravan	6	Post office
2	Bumpy road	7	Road
3	Trees	8	Telephone box
4	Shop (with red liquorice)	9	Stile
		10	Turnstile
5	Entrance		

Using some story cubes, he was able to come up with several other experiences in under a minute. If you roll a story cube and ask, 'What does this remind me of?' Your brain will come back with an answer (remember, it's like Google!) and offer up an experience connected to it. In this way you can create literally thousands of files – by simply probing your brain.

The main topics you use are completely up to you, but here are a few key ones to get you started:

▶ Events   ▶ Things

▶ People   ▶ Time

▶ Places

THE JOURNEY SYSTEM

In this activity you will aim to create 50 new files using the journey system.

Your journey is the memory network; the memory files are locations along that journey. Numbers are not important: it is only the sequence of locations along the journey that is significant.

Follow these steps to create your own journey system mind map:

▶ **Start by drawing a central picture in the space below.**

▶ **Create some main branches using the main topics above, or create your own.**

- ▶ Use only one word per branch to hone your thoughts.
- ▶ Talk aloud to activate your various auditory systems.
- ▶ Let your mind drift back in time as you focus on each of the main branches.
- ▶ Add more branches as you come up with different experiences; each experience should remind you of a place.

- ▶ Choose a **place** and map out a **journey,** pulling out **locations** for your mental files.
- ▶ Create 50 files in the space below.

LIMITLESS

This exercise takes the idea of our brain being the Internet and memory networks being websites one step further. It uses a real website to help us create memory networks.

Even though you can create thousands of files just by searching your brain, it's good to have other ways of creating memory networks. This is where Google Streetview can add to value to your toolbox, allowing you to create virtually limitless memory networks and files.

Follow these steps to create your first virtual memory network:

- ▶ Go to the following location in Google Streetview: http://goo.gl/maps/vTtTY – BBC New Broadcasting House in London.
- ▶ Create ten files by doing a 360-degree sweep (do two chunks of five in the same way you would for a memory palace).
- ▶ Move five clicks up the street and create ten files – click here: http://goo.gl/maps/Iqc6k
- ▶ Do another five clicks and create ten more files – click here: http://goo.gl/maps/kfMbD

By using this simple strategy, you can easily create an almost limitless number of files.

→ Mixed combinations

Now that you have a good understanding of how to use creative memorization to produce chains and networks, the opportunity for designing a complex mix of chains and networks opens up.

Think back to Exercise 29, Creative chains. What would happen if you associated the first item of each of those four chains to a memory file on the Google journey you just created? Let us imagine that the first four memory files were: Pillars, Clock, Tree and Hotel. Then you could associate:

- ▶ Prepare with Pillars
- ▶ Presentation with Clock
- ▶ Practise with Tree
- ▶ Performance with Hotel

Now, whenever you think about the Pillars (your first memory file on this memory network), you remember the image for prepare which in turn sparks off images for arousal, interest, goal, benefits, etc.

How you decide to mix your networks, chains or reference stories will depend on your purpose.

Exercise 36

REAL-LIFE APPLICATIONS

Think about some of the things you want to achieve in your life with a more effective memory. How could you use memory networks or chain methods to help you? Write down your ideas on a mind map or make some visual notes below.

Choose one or more of the following tasks you can do in the next 24 hours:

☐ To-do list

☐ Shopping list

☐ Ideas for a presentation

☐ Something else:

_____

_____

_____

Summary

In this chapter you have used a variety of creative memorization strategies to remember over 160 items and create more than 80 memory files. As a final challenge, see how many of those items you can recite aloud.

What I have learned

→ What are my thoughts, feelings and insights on what I have read so far?

_____

_____

_____

Use the space below to summarize the actions to take as a result of reading this chapter.

_____

_____

_____

_____

Where to next?

In the next chapter you will explore some key concepts in accelerated learning and how they connect with creative memorization. You will then be able to set yourself up to make yourself smarter by improving your memory.

5 Accelerated learning

When I was ten, I remember getting a physics and chemistry set, learning about the various chemicals, creating circuit boards and experimenting! Once I got so carried away, testing out my ideas, that I blew up the chemistry set and there were pieces of goo stuck to my goggles and to the ceiling. My dad walked in, looked at me, glanced around the room, gave an 'Oh boy!' kind of look and walked out again. Five years later, however, my 15-year-old self pretty much hated physics and chemistry; for some reason, the way I learned these subjects at school had knocked the fun and wonder of them out of me.

> '*Live as if you were to die tomorrow. Learn as if you were to live forever.*'
>
> Mahatma Gandhi

→ A learning experience

It was the night before my physics exam and I was cramming. My parents had made a deal with me that, if I passed all my exams, I could try out for a performing arts school in London. I was definitely primed and emotionally motivated, even though I had failed the mock exams before Christmas and my science teachers were not hopeful that I would pass.

All the odds were against me but, even though it was a subject I now had little interest in, I was determined to pass. I needed a strategy and I had 24 hours to create one. It was going to be a long night.

Unbeknown to me, I proceeded to take an accelerated learning approach:

1 My **goal** was clear and I understood the **benefits** I would reap if I followed through. I pulled together textbooks, exam notes, books from experiments and turned my parents' kitchen into a lab – I think my parents decided to have an early night.

2 I created a set of **activities** based on what I thought would take me from an E to a C grade. This consisted of memorizing about 20 different equations, **reflecting** on experiments I had done with them and **practising** how I might use them in the **context** of a question.

3 Before knowing anything about memory strategies, I had an **image** that represented each equation, **chunked** these up into categories, **wrote** them on flash cards and **rehearsed** where I would put them into practice.

4 I **tested** them out using an old exam paper to get a sense of how they would work in the **real world**. For the first time in about three years I was actually **excited** about physics!

5 In the morning, before going to the exam, I remember **talking** with my **friends**, sharing my strategy with them, and this reinforced my learning as I **articulated** how I could put each equation into **practice** and how I would recognize when to use the appropriate one.

6 For the first time ever, I felt I was walking into the exam with a handful of notes in front of me. I was confident I could achieve my goal…

Come the summer this goal was realized: I had passed with a C. Who knows what would have happened had I had 48 hours instead of 24. What was interesting was that I thought I would immediately forget everything after the exam, but the opposite happened. The equations stayed with me for months. I may even have tried to block some of them out! The activities I went through had been visual (learning through seeing), auditory (learning through talking and hearing), somatic (learning through doing and feeling) and they stimulated my intellect by making me reflect on what I knew and come up with ideas of how to put them into practice.

Years later, after reading numerous books in the field of differentiated learning, including David Kolb's *Experiential Learning*, James Zull's *The Art of Changing the Brain*, David Meier's *Accelerated Learning* and Howard Gardner's *Frames of Mind*, on his theory of multiple intelligences, I realized that being able to adapt to a learning style was a theme that seemed to connect these ideas.

Exercise 37

THE LEARNING CYCLE

Read the following account of two siblings and how it might relate to the image below.

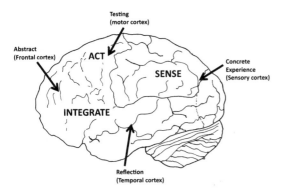

Aspects of the learning cycle

When working with a brother and sister, I noticed that they had different strengths.

The brother was great at observing and remembering facts but less good at bringing those facts together, seeing the big picture, organizing his own thoughts and taking action on them.

The sister, on the other hand, was the opposite: she had good high-level understanding, could see the big picture and how things fitted together, and she could propose actions to take. However, she lacked the ability to recall facts to back up her hypothesis.

Note down below how you think the siblings differ in the way they use the learning cycle.

_____

_____

_____

_____

Now read these simplified definitions of each part of the learning cycle:

▶ **Concrete experience:** Get curious to heighten your senses; what is interesting?

▶ **Reflective observation:** What does it remind you of? What does it mean to me? Use metaphors, similes and analogies.

- ▶ **Abstract hypothesis:** Become an explorer and director. How can you use this? What's the big picture? How does it fit together? What are the challenges?
- ▶ **Testing:** Act, rehearse, write, move, speak, get feedback and create a concrete experience.
- ▶ Use your **emotions** to motivate you.

This is how the siblings applied the learning cycle to improve their learning experience:

The brother was great at integrating facts (reflective observation); the sister was great at big-picture thinking and creating her own ideas (abstract hypothesis). Sharing a mind-mapping strategy with her brother helped him to guide and organize his thinking better, see the big picture and look for a course of action. Using some creative memorization strategies allowed the sister more easily to store data and facts to be recalled and used at a later date. In this way, both brother and sister started to fully utilize the learning cycle.

How would you use the learning cycle to remember the word *nublado*, Spanish for cloudy? Capture your thoughts in the space below.

→ How do you like to learn?

When you think of how you like to learn, do you instinctively have a preference? Are you a visual person who likes to learn by observing and imagining? Are you an auditory person who likes to learn by listening, using repetition and talking things through? Or are you a kinaesthetic person who likes to get up and do stuff, working things out until you get a feeling for what it's all about? If you had to pick the first one of these preferences that came into your head, which one would it be?

IDENTIFYING YOUR LEARNING STYLE

Try this simple exercise to identify your primary learning style. Ideally, do this with a partner or friend; if you do it on your own, make sure you talk aloud.

Think of something you want to achieve about six months from now. Start describing your goal in as much detail as possible, picking a specific scene in the future where things are going exactly as you planned. After you have given an overview of what you imagine yourself achieving, describe the scene in the following three different ways. Take up to two minutes for each description.

- ▶ **Visual – the things you see:** Include people, their expressions, actions, behaviour, colours, shapes, light, dark, shadows and anything else that comes up.

- ▶ **Auditory – the things you hear and the things you say:** Describe what people are saying to you, their tone of voice and how you are responding.

- ▶ **Kinaesthetic – the things you are doing and feeling:** Is it warm or cool, is music playing, what do you feel as you talk and listen to people, what are your emotions? Experience and describe this in as much detail as possible.

If you are with a friend or partner, ask them to do go through the same process of picking a goal and describing it in the same three ways.

Now do the following things:

→ Rate which of your partner's descriptions – visual, auditory or kinaesthetic – was easiest for you to follow.

→ Rate which of your descriptions– visual, auditory or kinaesthetic – was easiest for you to describe.

→ Overall, what would you rate as your dominant learning style?

→ What would be second?

→ What would be third?

Visual, auditory or kinaesthetic – write them in order below:

1 _____

2 _____

3 _____

→ Being SAVI

David Meier developed the SAVI model, an approach that optimizes learning. It has these components:

▶ **Somatic** – moving or doing (think kinaesthetic and hands on)

▶ **Auditory** – talking or hearing (think dialogue and debate)

▶ **Visual** – observing or picturing (think real-world examples, maps and diagrams)

▶ **Intellectual** – problem solving and questioning (think engaged, strategic, creative)

Meier describes the last element in SAVI, intellectual, as 'what learners do in their minds internally as they exercise their intelligence to reflect on experience and to create connections'. You can see the connections between this and the learning cycle. Emotion and intuition are also key in the intellectual space, in order to build meaning and understanding.

Knowing what your dominant learning style is can give you ways to filter what you are learning through the appropriate sense, so as to better understand and remember. If you can build on this to create learning experiences that are SAVI, learning can be optimized. This idea is reflected in creative memorization where, in order to bring an image to life so that it is memorable, you aim to incorporate as many of your senses as possible, add in emotion and give it meaning so you can transfer it into your mid- to long-term memory.

Exercise 39

DESIGNING YOUR LEARNING

Even though they are aimed mainly at creating learning experiences for others, you can use SAVI principles to create learning experiences for yourself. This is a great model for naturally putting the learning cycle into practice. You can make use of creative memorization and as many activities as you can think of.

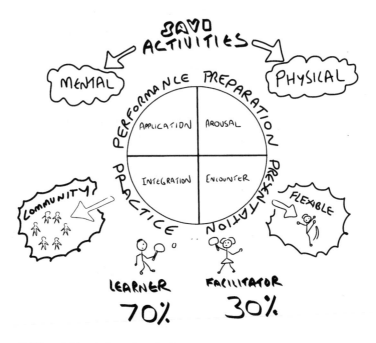

SAVI activities in learning design

- ▶ Study the picture on the previous page and come up with a view of what each element means.
- ▶ Think back to the chains you created in Exercise 29, Creative chains, for example the sequence of Preparation, Arousal, Interest, Goal, Benefits, etc. Each one of those four chains represents key ideas for each phase of rapid instructional design:

  a) **Preparation:** there should be an **arousal** of **interest** and a clear **goal**, the **benefits** should be understood and bought into, and there should be a positive, **physical, emotional** and **social** environment. Offer positive **suggestions** about the content, calm any **fears**, lower any **barriers** and get everyone **involved** from the very beginning.

  b) **Presentation:** look for **encounters** where you can **collaborate** and **observe**, a good mix of **brain** and **body interactive** activities, use **colour** to stimulate, classify and attract, play to all learning **styles**, making sure it's SAVI, set **projects** to undertake that have exploration and **discovery** at their heart, put in context of real-**world** examples and pose **problems** to solve.

  c) **Practice: integrate** activities that give time for **processing** information – reflecting and abstracting thoughts, **trial** and feedback, **simulations** of real events, **games** that offer challenge and reward, **activities** that allow time to **articulate** ideas and solutions, **dialogue** and discussion, opportunity for **teaching** and passing on **skills**.

  d) **Performance: plan** how to **apply** what has been learned, **reinforcing** knowledge and skills, and creating **materials** that support information. After a session there may be a need for some ongoing **coaching**, further **evaluation** of success, some **peer** review or – depending on the context – changes needed at an **organizational** level to support future growth.

- ▶ Think of presentation and practice like a game of tennis, where the facilitator is creating the space for the learner to integrate.
- ▶ SAVI activities should alternate between physical and mental, and include a mix of individual, partner and community. If you are working on your own, try to get feedback and opinions.
- ▶ Be flexible, learn from what works and what doesn't and say what you'll do to improve the next time.

Use these principles to design a 15-minute experience you could share with a friend that would show them how to use creative memorization, the chain method and a memory network in a real-world situation.

→ Outline one or two benefits (preparation):

_____

_____

→ Create three simple SAVI activities (presentation/practice):

_____

_____

_____

→ Identify where they could be used in the real world (performance):

_____

_____

Capture your design in the space below. Give yourself no more than 15 minutes and start with the activities, one of which should be physical.

→ Multiple intelligences

Thomas Armstrong based his idea that there are seven different ways a person can be smart (*7 kinds of smart*) on Howard Gardner's theory of multiple intelligences. This theory proposes different types of intelligence and that they can be applied in different ways.

The idea of multiple intelligences offers a useful way of looking at how a better memory could help you perform smarter. Gardner includes the linguistic, musical, logical–mathematical, spatial, bodily–kinaesthetic and personal as different types of intelligence, but for the purposes of framing where creative memorization can help performance I have used the following terms: word, music, number, picture, body and emotion.

MEMORY SMARTS

The following table shows six areas where a better memory can make you smarter. Tick any of the areas where you would like to perform better:

Memory for word smarts		Memory for music smarts	
Increasing vocabulary	☐	Getting into the flow	☐
Learning new languages	☐	Remembering sequences	☐
Using the right terminology	☐	Music for lyrics	☐
Presenting with confidence	☐	Bringing back memories	☐
Remembering quotes and speeches	☐	Conversations about music	☐
Memory for number smarts		**Memory for picture smarts**	
Helping kids with numbers	☐	Remembering events	☐
Remembering PINs, phone numbers, extensions	☐	Remembering directions	☐
Using statistics and research	☐	Diagrams, maps and how things fit	☐
Remembering key dates and facts	☐	Where you left things	☐
Remembering equations or formulae	☐	Creating visual cues	☐
Memory for body smarts		**Memory for emotional smarts**	
Picking up physical sequences	☐	Beliefs about your memory	☐
Dancing	☐	Remembering names and details	☐
Martial arts	☐	Recalling conversations	☐
Pilates/yoga	☐	Solving problems	☐
Sports	☐	Influencing through evidence	☐

 *Exercise 41*

PERFORMING

Make a mark on each of the scales below at the point where you believe you are now in your ability to perform at your best and achieve results.

→ Your career:

1 _____ 10

→ Your business:

1 _____ 10

→ Your relationships:

1 _____ 10

→ Your money

1 _____ 10

→ Your health:

1 _____ 10

→ Your body:

1 _____ 10

If you could rapidly accelerate the rate at which you could master the areas you ticked in Exercise 40, using creative memorization and accelerated learning strategies, what difference do you think it would make to your performance? Put a second mark on the above scales.

Summary

In this chapter you have put the learning cycle into practice, gained an understanding of accelerated learning principles and started your journey to performing smarter with your memory.

What I have learned

→ What are my thoughts, feelings and insights on what I have read so far?

_____

_____

_____

Use the space below to summarize the actions to take as a result of reading this chapter.

_____

_____

_____

_____

Where to next?

In the following chapters you will continue to use creative memorization to perform smarter in six key areas of intelligence: words, numbers, music, pictures, the body and the emotions.

6

Memory for word smarts

- -

In this chapter you will learn:

▶ ways to increase your vocabulary
▶ how to learn new languages
▶ techniques for remembering terminology and quotations
▶ how to present with confidence.

- -

Whether spoken or written, good linguistic skills are held in high regard in our society. From knowing the right words to use to influence a person or a group, to excelling at interviews, the words you use implicitly communicate something about you.

How can a better memory make you smarter with words? More specifically, how can you use creative memorization to improve your performance in areas where words are important? This chapter will take you through a number of memory activities that aim to improve your linguistic prowess.

'*All words are pegs to hang ideas on.*'

Henry Ward Beecher

Exercise 42

YOUR MAP OF WORDS

Choose someone at the top of their game in terms of their linguistic intelligence – a Stephen Fry, for example. Imagine that they are a ten on the scale below. Relative to this person, make three marks on the scale, to indicate:

▶ your current ability
▶ your potential
▶ your goal for the next three months.

Words:

1 _____ 10

Think about what it would mean to be smarter with words:

▶ **What would happen if you could increase your performance by 10–50 per cent?**
▶ **How would this make you feel?**
▶ **What current challenges do you face?**

Focusing on the questions above, spend no more than five minutes capturing your thoughts visually, using a mind map or notes, in the space below. Try to use single words that you can play back verbally.

→ Words and emotion

We instinctively know that words carry meaning and can affect how a person feels. What do you feel when you think about these words?

Happy	Exuberant	Rapturous
Euphoric	Gratified	Gleeful

Do they all make you 'feel' the same? It's unlikely, even though, by definition, they all describe 'happy' feelings to differing degrees. They show that the word you use to describe a feeling can have an effect on the emotion you experience. What do you feel like when you say, 'That makes me angry' compared with 'That makes me furious' or 'I'm livid'?

When you are angry or sad, try changing the word to 'splenetic' or 'doleful' and see what it does to your state. By expanding the number of words you have available to describe emotion, you take more control over how certain feelings affect you and therefore the decisions you make. Increasing your emotional vocabulary in this way will also prime your brain to look out for similar words.

Exercise 43

EMOTIVE WORDS

This exercise aims to recreate the physiology and feelings that go along with each word, so it's best to stand up when doing it.

▶ Create an image for each word.
▶ Associate your chain, writing in the table below.
▶ Say the words aloud.

Happy: Exuberant, Rapturous, Euphoric, Gratified, Gleeful	**Sad:** Crestfallen, Woebegone, Disconsolate, Doleful, Dejected
Chain:	Chain:
Grateful: Beholden, Appreciative, Indebted, Obliged, Thankful	**Angry:** Irate, Incensed, Exasperated, Indignant, Splenetic
Chain:	Chain:

Excited: Exhilarated, Enthusiastic, Animated, Stimulated, Eager	**Distressed:** Perturbed, Uptight, Dismayed, Discomposed, Uptight
Chain:	**Chain:**
Courageous: Indomitable, Valiant, Audacious, Intrepid, Valorous	**Worried:** Apprehensive, Disquieted, Perturbed, Agonized, Overwrought
Chain:	**Chain:**

A WORD JOURNAL

Over the next three days, look for opportunities to put the words from the previous exercise into practice. Rather than saying happy, excited, sad, down, pick an alternative and capture any changes or differences you notice. Record your findings below.

Day 1	Day 2	Day 3

→ Vocabulary blocks

This could be one of those sections of the workbook that you look at and think 'I'll come back to this later,' or 'That looks complex, it's going to take ages.' However, this part is *essential* if you want to become smarter with words. It's like buying a Lego set – not the kind you get when you're 5 or 6 years old but the 12+ kind. In order to enjoy it, you first have to become familiar with all the small components – the small glass lights, the handles, and the attachments for levers and wheels. You will usually then follow the instructions and build what's on the box.

Constructing something you can play with forms the big picture and allows you to see all those bits and pieces in action and how they fit together. When you buy your next new box of Lego, you'll be much more familiar with all the bits and pieces, which means that you can work out how things fit together a lot more quickly.

Words are no different. The components here are the bits and pieces that make up words (prefixes, roots and suffixes). Once you have a better understanding of what these do and how they construct words, you'll quickly start to recognize the meanings those words convey.

Here is a table of some of the prefixes, roots and suffixes used to construct words.

Word	Prefix	Root	Suffix	Meaning
Concurrence	con: with	curr: run	ence: act of	Act of running with, happening at same time
Exaggerate	ex: out	ag: to do, act	—	To act out
Irreversible	ir: not; re: again	vers: turning	ible: able to	Not able to turn back
Malediction	male: bad	dict: to say	—	To say bad things, a negative statement or curse
Precursor	pre: before	curs: to run	or: one who	One who runs before, something that comes before
Unity	uni: one	—	ty: state of	State of being one, a single thing or being
Untenable	un: not	ten: holding	able: able to	Not able to hold on

To accelerate the process of becoming familiar with these prefixes, roots and suffixes, you can apply the principles of creative memorization. The following exercises guide you through this process, to help create momentum; sample reference stories have been given for the first ten prefixes.

⏰ *Exercise 45*

GET THE ROOT

There are many ways you could use creative memorization to accelerate the process of getting this information into your body so you can start to use it. Here is one method, but feel free to design your own method using any creative memorization strategy. Your goal is to use the minimum number of images necessary to memorize the following prefixes, roots and suffixes and their meanings.

▶ Create a memory network with 32 files (real or virtual).

▶ Create a reference story incorporating the prefix/root/suffix, its meaning and the example word.

▶ Associate to a memory file.

▶ Dial up and talk through the meaning aloud (this is essential!).

Prefix	Meaning	Example word	Reference stories
a, ab, abs	away from	Absent	Someone with a great set of **abs**, **absent** from school
ad, a, ac, af, ag, an, ar, at, as	to, towards	Attract	**DR aNTS CoFFiNG** (letters d, c, f, g, n, r, t, s) attracted **towards** the fire
anti	against	Antisocial	An antisocial **ant** pushes **against** the crowd
bi, bis	two	Bicycle	A **bison** riding a **bicycle** with **two** large wheels
circum, cir	around	Circumscribe	A **circle** that is **circumscribed** around a triangle
com, con, co, col	with, together	Combine	**Combine** your friends' **Con**tacts **with** your **Co**-workers so it's easy to **Col**lect everyone **together**
de	away from, down, the opposite of	Depart	The **opposite** side of the track waiting to **depart**
dis, dif, di	apart	Distant	The **distant** relationship was pulling him **apart**
epi	upon, on top of	Epitaph	It read 'on top of the world' **upon** his **epitaph**
equ, equi	equal	Equalize	Two sticks of equal size

100

Prefix	Meaning	Example word	Reference stories
ex, e, ef	out, from	Exit	
in, il, ir, im, en	in, into	Inject	
in, il, ig, ir, im	not	Irreversible	
inter	between, among	International	
mal, male	bad, ill, wrong	Malfunction	
mis	wrong, badly	Mistreat	
mono	one, alone, single	Monopoly	
non	not, the reverse of	Nonsense	
ob	in front, against	Obstacle	
omni	everywhere, all	Omnipotent	
per	through	Perceive	
poly	many	Polygon	
post	after	Postmortem	
pre	before, earlier than	Prehistoric	
pro	going ahead of, supporting	Process	
re	again, back	Recede	
se	apart	Seclude	
sub	under, less than	Submarine	
super	over, above, greater	Superman	
trans	across	Transcontinental	
un, uni	one	Unidirectional	
un	not	Unethical	

Create a network of 27 files to remember the following roots.

Root	Meaning	Example word	Reference stories
act, ag	to do, to act	Agent	
apert	open	Aperture	
bas	low	Basement	
cap, capt, cip, cept, ceive	to take, to hold, to seize	Captive	
ced, cede, ceed, cess	to go, to give in	Access	
cred, credit	to believe	Incredible	
curr, curs, cours	to run	Current	
dic, dict	to say	Dictionary	
duc, duct	to lead	Aqueduct	
equ	equal, even	Equality	
fac, fact, fic, fect, fy	to make, to do	Factory	
fer, ferr	to carry, bring	Referral	
graph	write	Graphite	
mit, mis	to send	Missile	
par	equal	Disparate	
plic	to fold, to bend, to turn	Implicate	
pon, pos, posit, pose	to place	Deposit	
scrib, script	to write	Subscription	
sequ, secu	to follow	Sequel	
spec, spect, spic	to appear, to look, to see	Specimen	

Root	Meaning	Example word	Reference stories
sta, stat, sist, stit, sisto	to stand, or make stand	Status	
tact	to touch	Tactile	
ten, tent, tain	to hold	Maintain	
tend, tens, tent	to stretch	Extend	
tract	to draw	Attract	
ven, vent	to come	Advent	
ver, vert, vers	to turn	Reverse	

Create a network of 23 files to remember the following suffixes.

Suffix	Meaning	Words	Reference stories
able, ible, ble	able to	Edible	
acious, cous, al	like, having the quality of	Nocturnal Vivacious	
ance, ancy	the act of, a state of being	Truancy	
ant, ent, er, or	one who	Creator	
ar, ary	connected with, related to	Beneficiary	
ence	quality of, act of	Existence	
ful	full of	Fearful	
ic, ac, il, ile	of, like, pertaining to	Acidic	
ion	the act or condition of	Correction	
ism	the practice of, support of	Patriotism	
ist	one who makes, does	Artist	
ity, ty, y	the state of, character of	Shifty	

Suffix	Meaning	Words	Reference stories
ive	*having the nature of*	*Active*	
less	*lacking, without*	*Heartless*	
logy	*the study of*	*Biology*	
ment	*the act of, the state of*	*Retirement*	
ness	*the quality of*	*Eagerness*	
ory	*having the nature of*	*Laboratory*	
ous, ose	*full of, having*	*Dangerous*	
ship	*the art or skill of, the ability to*	*Leadership*	
some	*full of, like*	*Troublesome*	
tude	*the state of, the ability to*	*Aptitude*	
y	*Full of, somewhat like*	*Chilly*	

If you have followed through on this activity, start looking for opportunities to put your knowledge into practice. This will reaffirm what you know and you will reap the rewards!

→ Words in your career

Whenever you begin a new role or career, there is usually some unfamiliar language or terminology. Depending on your profession, there could be vast amounts. Having instant access to this language can be a quick-fire way to build up domain knowledge and become a potential go-to person.

 BUSINESS TERMS

Using creative memorization, remember the following business terms and their definitions.

Business term	Reference story
AIDA – Attention, Interest, Desire, Action – an early and fundamentally useful model/process for effective communications. We all buy things after passing through these four key stages.	*Example:* A first AIDer giving Attention, Interest, Desire and Action to a sick letter A
Bootstrapping – starting a business from scratch and building it up with minimum outside investment.	
Business plan – a written document which sets out a business's plans and objectives, and how it will achieve them, e.g. by marketing, development, production, etc.	
Competitor analysis – a company's marketing strategy, which involves assessing the performance of competitors in order to determine their strengths and weaknesses.	
Eyeballs – an advertising term. A name given to the number of people who visit a website advertisement, which can be counted by the number of click-throughs.	
Gap analysis – enables a company to assess the gap between its actual performance and its potential performance, by comparing what skills, products, etc., are available to what is required to improve performance.	
Maslow's Hierarchy of Needs – developed by Abraham Maslow in 1943. A fundamental motivational theory describing five stages of human needs, which must be met in a particular order: Biological, Safety, Belonging, Self-Esteem, Self-actualization.	
Pareto Principle – also known as the 80–20 Rule: e.g. 20% of employees perform 80% of the work; 20% of customers produce 80% of the revenue; or 80% of the required content is in 20% of the book.	
Qualitative – associated with a thing's quality, which cannot be measured, such as feel, image, taste, etc. Also describes people's qualities that cannot be measured.	
Quantitive – related to or measured in numbers, a comparison based on quantity rather than quality.	

LEARNING ANOTHER LANGUAGE

Use a similar three-step process to expand your vocabulary in a different language. In the same way that you learned language as a child, i.e. pointing to something and saying the word, try to use the word in context when learning a new language. Once you have created an image for the word, use your iMind to create a scene around you and physically point, grab and touch the things you are describing out loud.

▶ Create an image for the key words, both English and the second language – Spanish in this example (the Spanish image should trigger the sound).

▶ Project it externally using your iMind.

▶ Physically create a scene and act it out.

For example, with the word *panadería* (bakery), imagine you are in a Spanish street with your face pushed up against the window of a bakery, looking at a Pan of Madeira cake and saying *'panadería'*. Don't just imagine it; make it real, as if you are there. With some repetition, try just doing the action, seeing the baker's and see if the word comes to mind.

For the word *corazón* (heart), imagine grabbing your heart while holding a cord thong!

For *nieve* (snow), imagine kneeling in the snow.

> A great resource for continuing to build your language skills is Memrise, co-founded by Ed Cooke, coach to Joshua Foer, author of *Moonwalking with Einstein* (Foer, 2011) – www.memrise.com

Calle – street	Deporte – sport	Arco iris – rainbow	Nublado – cloudy	Día de descanso – holiday
Peluquería – barber shop	Semáforo – traffic lights	Esposa – wife	Patinaje – skating	Verdulería – greengrocer
Dorado – golden	Corazón – heart	Hoy – today	Lluvia – rain	Esposo – husband
Ida – one way	Perro – dog	Salida – departure	Aparcamiento – parking	Pájaro – bird
Conejo – rabbit	Mariposa – butterfly	Burro – donkey	Pez – fish	Semana – week
Carnicería – butcher shop	Nieve – snow	Panadería – bakery	Llegada – arrival	Hermanas – sister
Tiempo – weather	Baile – dancing	Morado – purple	Verano – summer	Estación – season
Plated – silver	Hermanos – brother	Mess – month	Cuerpo – body	Ayer – yesterday

Test out your recall by pointing to random squares on the following grid and saying the Spanish equivalent. As you play this game, keep your finger moving, never letting it stop. If you can't remember a word, let your finger move to the next square. Start with a slow pace and then build up speed as you become more familiar with the words.

Butterfly	Month	Summer	Sport	Skating
Arrival	Weather	Heart	Parking	Week
Husband	Season	Silver	Brother	Greengrocer
Departure	Butcher shop	Golden	Fish	Rain
Yesterday	Body	Bird	Sister	Bakery
Street	Purple	Dancing	Barber shop	Rainbow
Donkey	Today	One way	Holiday	Wife
Snow	Dog	Cloudy	Traffic lights	Rabbit

→ Presenting with confidence

What are your thoughts about speaking in public? For many it can be utter horror, while others relish the idea. Whether you are either of these extremes or somewhere in between, having the facility to deliver your core message without missing details, losing your way or completely freezing can transform your confidence.

 ## STORYBOARDS

Thinking about what you have covered so far in this workbook, draw a simple storyboard below with ten pictures or single words. They should represent **key points** you could talk about for 30 seconds each.

To get this presentation into your body:

▶ create a set of visual cues (these are the individual pictures in your storyboard)

▶ use your iMind to project those visual cues into the room (you should be able to go back and forth at speed and stay 'present' when you use your iMind in this scenario)

▶ rehearse 'as if' you were doing the real thing

▶ get into a state of flow

▶ find a friend and share with them what you have learned so far.

What could you do to put this skill into practice in different situations over the next three weeks? Write your ideas in the space below.

_____

_____

_____

→ The right words

Sometimes you need to know more than just the main topics for a presentation. You may have to learn a whole script word for word, or recite legislation or law verbatim. In order to do this, you are still going to need a good deal of rehearsal, but with creative memorization and taking a SAVI approach you can get those words into your body at a much quicker pace.

As an actor for 15 years, my ability to remember scripts word for word was of paramount importance. There are many different approaches you can take to remembering words verbatim. Reading something over and over again is one, which, unsurprisingly, can be quite painful. Rather than thinking about this as a set of steps, here is a recipe I have used in the past. As with all recipes, feel free to adapt and change it to suit you.

Think about what the following means to you. The key ingredients include:

▶ your intent
▶ the meaning
▶ any emotions
▶ physical actions
▶ creative visual cues.

Once you have those in place:

▶ prepare the words in your own language
▶ add in the words in their language
▶ cook it up for the appropriate amount of time
▶ serve with gusto!

Even though it is not necessary to write your inner workings down as reference stories, you may find that, as part of this exercise, it helps in keeping up momentum and crafting your stories.

Exercise 49

USING QUOTES

How might you adapt the recipe of key ingredients described above to serve up some of these tasty quotes?

1 **'Don't cry because it's over, smile because it happened.' – Dr Seuss**

Example: Your best friend got sacked, they are *crying* (visual cue) and bent *over* (visual cue). Hand them a photograph; they *smile* (visual cue). Act out in your own words, 'No need to cry; you loved that job', become Dr Seuss and – in his words – 'Don't cry because it's over, smile because it happened.'

2 **'Love looks not with the eyes, but with the mind.' – William Shakespeare**

Example: Juliet with her *eyes* closed, *thinking* of Romeo. In your words, 'She loves him, even though he is not here.' As Shakespeare, 'Love looks not with the eyes, but with the mind.'

3 **'Without music, life would be a mistake.' – Friedrich Nietzsche**

Example: a *dead broken guitar*… In your words, 'My music is dead, life's a mistake.' As Nietzche, 'Without music, life would be a mistake.'

4 **'The person, be it gentleman or lady, who has not pleasure in a good novel, must be intolerably stupid.' – Jane Austen**

Example: a *gentleman* and *lady* reading a Terry Pratchett *novel* and tutting *stupidly*. In your words, 'How can this man and woman not like this? Are they stupid?' As Jane, 'The person, be it gentleman or lady, who has not pleasure in a good novel, must be intolerably stupid.'

5 **'If you can't explain it to a six-year-old, you don't understand it yourself.' – Albert Einstein**

Example: trying to *explain* the *theory of relativity* (unsuccessfully) to your *child*. In your words, 'I can't explain this, I don't understand it.' As Einstein, 'If you can't explain it to a six-year-old, you don't understand it yourself.'

6 'You've gotta dance like there's nobody watching, love like you'll never be hurt, sing like there's nobody listening, and live like it's heaven on earth.' – William W. Purkey

7 'A room without books is like a body without a soul.' – Marcus Tullius Cicero

8 'In three words I can sum up everything I've learned about life: it goes on.' – Robert Frost

9 'Live as if you were to die tomorrow. Learn as if you were to live forever.' – Mahatma Gandhi

10 'I've learned that people will forget what you said, people will forget what you did, but people will never forget how you made them feel.' – Maya Angelou

11 'There are two ways to live your life. One is as though nothing is a miracle. The other is as though everything is a miracle.' – Albert Einstein

12 'Yesterday is history, tomorrow is a mystery, today is a gift of God, which is why we call it the present.' – Bil Keane (adapted in *Kung Fu Panda*!)

13 'I am enough of an artist to draw freely upon my imagination. Imagination is more important than knowledge. Knowledge is limited. Imagination encircles the world.' – Albert Einstein

14 'I have not failed. I've just found 10,000 ways that won't work.' – Thomas A. Edison

15 'You have brains in your head. You have feet in your shoes. You can steer yourself any direction you choose. You're on your own. And you know what you know. And *you* are the one who'll decide where to go...' – Dr Seuss

16 'For every minute you are angry you lose 60 seconds of happiness.' – Ralph Waldo Emerson

17 'Being deeply loved by someone gives you strength, while loving someone deeply gives you courage.' – Lao Tzu

18 'Logic will get you from A to Z; imagination will get you everywhere.' – Albert Einstein

19 'The trouble with having an open mind, of course, is that people will insist on coming along and trying to put things in it.' – Terry Pratchett

20 'It is impossible to live without failing at something, unless you live so cautiously that you might as well not have lived at all – in which case, you fail by default.' – J. K. Rowling

Let's see how well you cooked them.

1 Who said 'Love looks not with the eyes, but with the mind'?

   a. Albert Einstein

   b. William Shakespeare

   c. Dr Seuss

2 What is Friedrich Nietzsche attributed with saying?

   a. 'Without music, life would be a mistake.'

   b. 'In three words I can sum up everything I've learned about life: it goes on.'

   c. 'Don't cry because it's over, smile because it happened.'

3 Which female author is quoted as saying, 'I've learned that people will forget what you said, people will forget what you did, but people will never forget how you made them feel'?

   a. Jane Austen

   b. J. K. Rowling

   c. Maya Angelou

4 What is Marcus Tullius Cicero quoted as saying?

   a. 'A room without books is like a body without a soul.'

   b. 'I have not failed. I've just found 10,000 ways that won't work.'

   c. 'I am enough of an artist to draw freely upon my imagination. Imagination is more important than knowledge. Knowledge is limited. Imagination encircles the world.'

5 'Yesterday is history, tomorrow is a mystery, today is a gift of God, which is why we call it the present.' Who said this?

   a. Mahatma Gandhi

   b. Bil Keane

   c. Thomas A. Edison

6 What is Lao Tzu quoted as saying?

   a. 'For every minute you are angry you lose 60 seconds of happiness.'

   b. 'There are two ways to live your life. One is as though nothing is a miracle. The other is as though everything is a miracle.'

   c. 'Being deeply loved by someone gives you strength, while loving someone deeply gives you courage.'

7 'You have brains in your head. You have feet in your shoes. You can steer yourself any direction you choose. You're on your own. And you know what you know. And *you* are the one who'll decide where to go...' Who said this?

a. Ralph Waldo Emerson

b. Dr Seuss

c. William W. Purkey

8 What did Albert Einstein say?

a. 'I am enough of an artist to draw freely upon my imagination. Imagination is more important than knowledge. Knowledge is limited. Imagination encircles the world.'

b. 'The trouble with having an open mind, of course, is that people will insist on coming along and trying to put things in it.'

c. 'I have not failed. I've just found 10,000 ways that won't work.'

9 Who said, 'It is impossible to live without failing at something, unless you live so cautiously that you might as well not have lived at all – in which case, you fail by default'?

a. Terry Pratchett

b. Dr Seuss

c. J. K. Rowling

10 Who said, 'The person, be it gentleman or lady, who has not pleasure in a good novel, must be intolerably stupid'?

a. Albert Einstein

b. Friedrich Nietzsche

c. Jane Austen

Summary

In this chapter you have explored the building blocks of vocabulary, acquired a process for memorizing terminology, learned how to remember vocabulary in other languages, discovered techniques for making a presentation with confidence and cooked up a creative memorization recipe for words.

Before moving on, go back to Exercise 42 and make a mark on your scale at the point where you believe you are now.

What I have learned

What are my thoughts, feelings and insights on what I have read so far?

_____

_____

_____

Use the space below to summarize the actions to take as a result of reading this chapter.

_____

_____

_____

_____

Where to next?

In the next chapter, you will uncover how creative memorization techniques can open up the language of numbers.

7 Memory for number smarts

In this chapter you will learn:
▶ strategies that make memorizing numbers as easy as pi
▶ how to remember phone numbers and extensions
▶ how to have credit cards and PINs at your fingertips
▶ ways to build your knowledge of statistics and dates.

How good is your short-term memory? Could you take a 20-digit number and remember it forwards and backwards in sequence after only 30 seconds, and retain it for days or even weeks, by doing it that one time? In this chapter you will learn strategies that will show you how.

'*Logic is the anatomy of thought.*'

John Locke

 Exercise 50

 TEST YOUR NUMBER MEMORY

Study the following number for 30 seconds – no longer.

7 8 2 1 6 3 7 4 9 5 3 1 8 0 1 4 2 0 3 9

▶ Cover the number.
▶ Stand up.
▶ Count out loud from 10 down to 1.
▶ Sit down.

In the box below, write as many of the digits – in sequence – as you can remember.

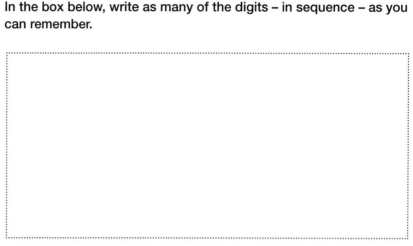

Most people will get around five correct in sequence before errors start to creep in. Anything more than 15 is exceptional.

→ # A world of numbers

What do you think of people who can readily pull statistics out of the air, recall key dates and know important financial figures? Does that sound off-putting, or are you already one of those people? In the same way as being smart with words can improve your capabilities in many areas of your life, improving your memory for numbers can make a big difference to how successful you are in your day-to-day life and career.

By expanding your capabilities, you will gain an edge over your competitors in business: knowledge of numbers brings with it kudos as well as the expertise to influence with evidence and gain buy-in from those who, although they may be interested in the vision, ultimately just want the facts.

Outside business and within social circles, having numerical data at your fingertips on favourite sports, authors and topics of interest can be a fun pursuit. Or perhaps you just want to impress your friends by memorizing their credit card numbers and then telling them you won't see them for a while, as you're off to Barbados for a month. That usually triggers a few chortles in terms of a party trick, shortly followed by, 'But wait a minute: you now know my credit card number – how long does that last?!' to which you reply, 'About a month…'

 *Exercise 51*

WHERE ARE YOU WITH NUMBERS?

Think of a person whom you regard as excellent with numbers. On a scale of 1 to 10, if they are a 10, where are you in terms of:

▶ your current ability?
▶ your potential?
▶ your goal for three months' time?

Mark your answers on the scale:

1_____10

Think about what it would mean to be smarter with numbers.

▶ What would happen if you could increase your performance by 10–50 per cent?
▶ How would this make you feel?
▶ What current challenges do you face?

Give yourself five minutes to assemble your thoughts. Use the space below to make notes, or use your note-taking tool of choice. Make sure you play back to yourself verbally what you write down.

REMEMBERING NUMBERS: THE BASICS

The first thing to do is give numbers more meaning so that they are easier for us to remember. If you have children, nephews, nieces or grandchildren, try this exercise with them and see how easy it is for them to remember number patterns through story.

If you were teaching your child to remember the seven times table, for example, you can create a reference for them that gives more meaning. You can suggest that they 'become' the number 7 – perhaps 007, a secret agent – then get them to go on a journey around their garden and give several locations a number:

▶ **The bush**

▶ **The roses**

▶ **The tree**

▶ **The grassy patch**

▶ **Under the fence, and so on...**

Tell a story to link each location, in the following way:

'In the bush they see a garden angel from Heaven, in the prickly roses they encounter a pencil with a door handle as a nose, the pencil warns them of dangers ahead, but the brave number 7 has no fear, twists the pencil's nose and walks through only to meet the Tree of Treasures, guarded by a bizarre-looking creature the natives call Swaney Bun...'

What you have done here is create a framework to accelerate the speed at which your child can remember the 7 times table:

▶ **Heaven sounds like 7.**

▶ **The pencil looks like a 1 and door rhymes with 4, that's 14.**

▶ **The swan looks like a 2 and bun rhymes with 1, that's 21.**

Think about the story again.

▶ **At the 1st place 7 met the angel from heaven 7: $1 \times 7 = 7$**

▶ **At the 2nd place 7 met the pencil 1 with a door 4 nose: $2 \times 7 = 14$**

▶ **At the 3rd place 7 met the swan 2 with a bun 1: $3 \times 7 = 21$**

Your child, who had no previous frame of reference, now has a language in which to understand the sequence of numbers in the table, with some repetition (but much less than if you were just to tell them to repeat the times table over and over again until it eventually sinks in). With this, the child starts to understand the 7 times table.

You can then combine this with writing them out, answering questions, dividing as well as multiplying. At this stage the story becomes much less important and after time will most likely not be referenced. It was only there to kick-start the process. While this number system is a great starter for children, it is limited, and we need something more elaborate as a strategy for an adult.

 Exercise 53

CREATING A LANGUAGE FOR NUMBERS

The aim of this exercise is to create a language for numbers, so that each number has a sound associated with it from which you can create words.

Set a timer for five minutes and study the following picture. Explore the image in detail, look for connections, form an opinion or take your best guess. Then talk it through aloud or discuss it with a friend.

What do you think the purpose of this image is?

How do you think you would put this into practice?

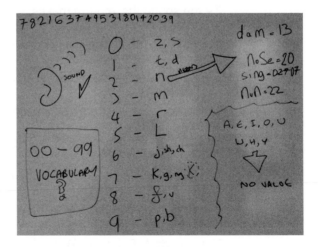

Notes on creating a language for numbers

Capture your thoughts in the space below.

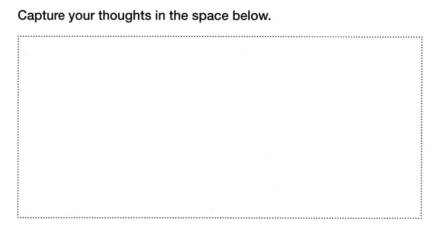

Did you figure it out? Our goal here is the same as in the previous system: to create a language for numbers, in this case a set of images that refer to every 2-digit number from 0 to 99. To do this there is a code, a phonetic system where each number from 0 to 9 has a 'sound' or set of 'sounds' associated with it. From these sounds you can create words.

The following represents the phonetic sounds associated with each number from 0 to 9:

0 – the sounds that the letters z and s make, as in Zorro and Snake.

1 – the sounds that the letters t and d make, as in Teddy and Diamond.

2 – the sound the letter n makes, as in Nuts.

3 – the sound the letter m makes, as in Mike.

4 – the sound the letter r makes, as in Rat.

5 – the sound the letter l makes, as in Light.

6 – the sounds the letters j, sh and ch make, as in Jam, Ship and Chips.

7 – the sounds the letters c, k, g and ng make, as in Cat, Gun and ring.

8 – the sounds the letters f and v make, as in Fire and Van.

9 – the sounds the letters p and b make, as in Pea and Bite.

The sounds A, E, I, O, U, W, H, Y have no value. These no-value sounds enable us to create words.

It is important to note that it is not the *name* of the letter but the *sound* of the letter that equates to the number, so the word CoFFee represents the number 78 and not 788 because the sound the FF makes is 'F, as in CoFee'.

In the examples on the picture:

▶ dam = 13   d is 1, a has no value, m is 3
▶ nose = 20   n is 2, o has no value, s is 0
▶ sing = 07   s is 0, i has no value, ng is 7
▶ nun = 22   n is 2, u has no value, n is 2.

Exercise 54

USING SOUND CARDS

A quick way to become familiar with this phonetic system is to play a simple card game. Aim to play it in one minute.

▶ Grab a pack of cards and remove all the picture cards. This will leave you with the number cards (1–10) in each suit; 10 will represent the number 0.
▶ Shuffle the number cards.
▶ When you are ready, start a stopwatch for a minute.
▶ Turn over the cards one by one.
▶ Out loud, say just one sound that each card makes.
▶ See how quickly you can get through the whole pack.

→ Your number matrix

Once you understand the phonetic system, you can begin designing your personalized number matrix from 00 to 99. It might look something like the one below. The words included are just examples. The number 20, for instance, could be **nose**, **NASA** or **niece**.

00 Sauce	01 Sit	02 Sin	03 Sam	04 Soar	05 Sail	06 Sash	07 Sack	08 Safe	09 Zip
10 Daisy	11 Data	12 Dan	13 Dam	14 Door	15 Doll	16 Dash	17 Duck	18 Toffee	19 Tap
20 Nose	21 Net	22 Nun	23 Nam	24 Nero	25 Nail	26 Nash	27 Nag	28 Knife	29 Nappy
30 Mace	31 Mat	32 Minnie	33 Mummy	34 Marry	35 Mail	36 Mash	37 Mag	38 Mafia	39 Map
40 Race	41 Rat	42 Rain	43 Rum	44 Roar	45 Rail	46 Rash	47 Rake	48 RAF	49 Rope
50 Lace	51 Lead	52 Alien	53 Lamb	54 Lara	55 Lilly	56 Lash	57 Lake	58 Leave	59 Lab
60 Jaws	61 Shot	62 Chain	63 Jam	64 Chair	65 Chilli	66 Gigi	67 Chuck	68 Chief	69 Chap
70 Case	71 Cat	72 Can	73 Gum	74 Car	75 Claw	76 Cash	77 Cake	78 Café	79 Cap
80 Face	81 Fat	82 Vine	83 Foam	84 Fur	85 Fool	86 Fish	87 Fag	88 Viva	89 Phebe
90 Boss	91 Bat	92 Bin	93 Beam	94 Beer	95 Ball	96 Bash	97 Bag	98 Beef	99 Poppy

Exercise 55

BREAKING THE CODE

Once you know which word represents which number, you can simply use a memory network or chain these words to remember a sequence of numbers. Using the above table, decode the following words:

café, net, jam, car, ball, mat, face, door, nose, map

Write the number in the space below:

_____

You'll recognize this as the number you memorized in the beginning of this chapter. By learning this system, you can open up a whole world of possibilities when it comes to your memory of numbers.

For this strategy to become useful, you will want to get to the point that you would with any language where you don't have to 'think' or go through a 'decode' process to remember what word a number is. When you see or hear 22, you should immediately be able to make a creative connection with the image of a NuN. In order for this to happen, you first need to become familiar with the code.

Exercise 56

LEARNING YOUR MEMORY MATRIX

There are many ways you could go about creating and learning your memory matrix. You could jump straight into number memorization, use flash cards or play number recognition games, where you print up the numbers 00 to 99 on a sheet of A3 paper and touch them randomly, saying the number they represent. These are all an excellent way to build up your speed and accuracy.

Here is a useful technique that uses a memory network and the chain method to embed the core images quickly in your mind.

▶ First, design 100 words that feel like a good fit for you (use the table below).
▶ Create a small memory network with just ten files.
▶ Use the chain method to memorize the images you have created for your number matrix in groups of 10; numbers 00 to 09, then 10 to19, 20 to 29 and so on, until you have 10 separate chains.

Here is an example:

'You are holding a giant bottle of sauce (00) while you sit (01) in a house of sin (02) with Sam (03) and soar (04) through space, powered by an atomic sail (05) made of a red satin sash (06), but you crash into a sack (07) and get locked in a safe (08) that is closed by a zip (09).'

Now use your memory network and place the first image of each chain on a separate file. Sauce (00) goes on file no. 1, Daz (10) goes on file no. 2, Nasa (20) goes on file no. 3.

The seven-day challenge: Over the next week, spend five minutes a day running through the matrix in your mind, saying the numbers aloud as you visualize the images. If you have trouble with any of the numbers, change that image to something that sticks.

	0	1	2	3	4	5	6	7	8	9
0										
10										
20										
30										
40										
50										
60										
70										
80										
90										

Numbers can be a memory strategy that stops people in their tracks. With your new skills what may seem like a small mountain is probably just a small hill. Follow through on this activity; it is much easier than it may first appear and will pay off for you in the long run.

→ Numbers in the real world

With data on smartphones and other devices now being stored in the Cloud, the need to remember phone numbers seems less and less important. But if backups fail, you lose the numbers you've built up in your store. You might meet someone ad hoc and need to keep their number in your head, until you can transfer it to a permanent device. And having work extension numbers in your head can also save you time – and therefore money – in the long run.

Similarly, most people look at their credit or bank card to check the number each time they place an online or phone order. Do you also have to double-check the three-digit code on the back of the card even though you've used it many times?

Having a good memory for statistics can also be useful. By understanding statistics, we increase our knowledge about how things relate to each other and their impact. Numbers give you context and they can tell a story, so backing up a conversation with statistics you've remembered can offer you extra credibility.

MEMORIZING EXTENSION NUMBERS

Memorize the following ten extensions and whose they are:

Jane	Elizabeth	Mark	Mary	John
5225	5218	5278	5216	5283
Pete	Jess	James	Toby	Alice
6193	6130	4857	4087	1828

For Jane, for example, you might imagine someone you know called Jane who is actually an alien (52) with bright green nails (25).

Cover the table above and write down, in the following diagram, the extension number for each person in the box containing their name.

MEMORIZING PINS AND BANK CARDS

Here's a simple way to lock your personal and business bank cards in your head to speed up the transaction process.

▶ Design a memory network that contains three memory files for each card you want to remember – you may decide to use a memory network in the bank of the relevant card.

▶ Chain the long number together and associate to memory file no. 1. Associate the expiration date to file no. 2.

▶ Associate the three-digit code to file no. 3.

Try this now and, the next time you use your card, do it by memory!

Exercise 59

MEMORIZING STATISTICS

Look at this mind map about brain statistics.

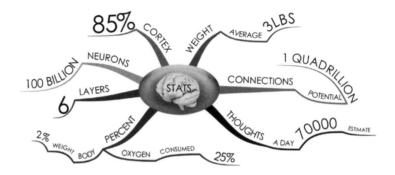

Statistics shown in a mind map

▶ Choose a method to memorize the facts it contains.

▶ Recreate these statistics in any form you like.

▶ Use it in a conversation tomorrow.

Now capture in the space below what statistics you could memorize on a continuous basis that would add value to your personal life or career.

REMEMBERING DATES

In the same way that statistics bring credibility to a conversation and tell a story, knowing when things happened can have the same impact. Being able to place events in a particular time gives them context, as well as making them memorable for the person or people you are talking to. It is sometimes not so much about the numbers as the stories the numbers tell.

Use the inventions you memorized in Exercise 22, this time adding the date into the mix. Simply increase your chain by adding in an image for the date. Enter the dates below.

Inventions and inventors	Date
Electric battery – Alessandro Volta	*1800*
Photography – Fox Talbot and Daguerre	
Miners' lamp – Humphry Davy	
Electromagnet – William Sturgeon	
Waterproof clothes – Charles Macintosh	
Microphone – Charles Wheatstone	
Lawn mower – Edwin Budding	
Refrigeration – Jacob Perkins	
Revolver – Samuel Colt	
Postage stamp – Rowland Hill	
Vacuum cleaner – Hubert Booth	
Traffic lights – J. P. Knight	

Summary

In this chapter you have begun to use a system that can give you easy access to the numbers in your life, from helping a child with times tables, to phone numbers, dates and statistics. Make sure you have created your chains for the number matrix and continue to pick up the seven-day challenge!

Before moving on, go back to Exercise 51 and mark the point on your scale where you believe you are now in your ability with numbers.

What I have learned

What are my thoughts, feelings and insights on what I have read so far?

_____

_____

_____

_____

Use the space below to summarize the actions to take as a result of reading this chapter.

_____

_____

_____

_____

Where to next?

In the next chapter you will experience what the world of music can do for your memory and how your memory can help you with music.

8

Memory for musical smarts

In this chapter you will learn:
- ▶ how to use music to unlock memories
- ▶ ways to enhance your memory for music conversations
- ▶ a way to prime yourself to listen more deeply
- ▶ how to use music to enhance memory for physical activity
- ▶ to create a memory playlist.

While writing or creating, I like to listen to music. Currently, my iTunes is on shuffle and a track just came on that I haven't listened to in years: the finale of a show I did back in 1994 in the West End of London, called *Crazy for You*. I am immediately transported back to the Prince Edward Theatre, singing and dancing in front of over 2,000 people, and the memories and emotions come flooding back.

Even as I write this, I have a big smile on my face, remembering the people I worked with during that time, their energy and enthusiasm. I can even remember some of the routines, and the lyrics of the songs are locked in my mind. As I think about the song 'I got rhythm', I get a surge of adrenaline through my body as I relive it in my mind. Music is indeed a powerful tool for bringing back memories.

Music can be great at putting you 'in the zone', as it evokes autobiographical memories by engaging the medial prefrontal cortex, which is what helps us make associations between context, locations, events and our emotional responses.

'In memory everything seems to happen to music.'

Tennessee Williams

Listening to music and identifying instruments can be a good way to heighten your ability to differentiate sounds and hone your musical ear. Being able to visualize things while you listen and then recreate what you visualize can bring a whole new dimension to your creative memorization.

Exercise 61

EXPLORING YOUR MUSICAL EXPERIENCE

In this exercise you will explore your experiences of music, with the goal of building up a picture of what music means to you and where it fits into your life.

When you think of music in your life, what memories come to mind? Brainstorm your ideas and create a timeline in the space below.

Match up any of the memories you brainstormed with any of the experiences below. Check the box and add details of the memory.

Music experiences	Memory
☐ Put you in a state of flow	
☐ Make you feel confident	
☐ Inspire you!	
☐ Help you learn	
☐ Good to read to	
Something else _____ _____	

Exercise 62

WHAT'S YOUR MUSICAL INTELLIGENCE?

When you think of someone with a strong musical intelligence, who comes to mind?

If this person represents a 10 on the scale below, where are you in terms of:

▶ your current ability?
▶ your potential?
▶ your goal in three months' time?

Mark the point where you think you are in terms of musical intelligence on the scale below.

1_____10

Exercise 63

HONING YOUR MUSICAL EAR

In this exercise you will practise honing your musical ear by listening to Prokofiev's *Peter and the Wolf*. Prokofiev was commissioned to write this musical symphony for children, and it was first performed in May 1936. This well-known and very visual composition is a story with both music and text by Prokofiev, spoken by a narrator and accompanied by the orchestra.

For a free download and streaming, go to: archive.org/details/PeterAndTheWolf_753

Read the notes in the box below and then listen to *Peter and the Wolf*. As you listen, aim to do three things:

▶ **Differentiate between the instruments.**

▶ **Let the music create visuals in your mind.**

▶ **Recreate some key moments after listening.**

Peter and the Wolf

Peter and the Wolf is scored for the following orchestra:

▶ Woodwind: a flute, an oboe, a clarinet in A and a bassoon

▶ Brass: three horns in F, a trumpet in B-flat and a trombone

▶ Percussion: timpani, a triangle, a tambourine, cymbals, castanets, a snare drum and a bass drum

▶ Strings: first and second violins, violas, violoncellos and double basses

Each character in the story has a particular instrument and a musical theme:

▶ Bird: flute

▶ Duck: oboe

▶ Cat: clarinet

▶ Grandfather: bassoon

▶ Wolf: horns

▶ Hunters: woodwind theme, with gunshots on timpani and bass drum

▶ Peter: stringed instruments

While this piece is a good one to start with, feel free to seek out more challenging pieces to improve your skills in this area.

Capture your experience in the space below.

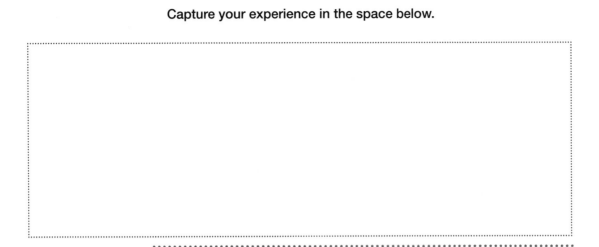

→ Using music in memorization

In the same way that you might build up a vocabulary for numbers, you can also build up a visual vocabulary for music. The purpose of this is to add another dimension to your creative memorization. For some people, bringing music or sounds into their chains or networks is a natural thing to do, while for others it can feel foreign. The following exercise will offer some trigger words that will help you practise your ability to incorporate sounds or music into your visualizations.

 *Exercise 64*

USING MUSIC TRIGGER WORDS

If you are musically inclined, this simple exercise can be a great way of sparking off images in your creative stories.

Memorize the following 20 words, using music that comes to mind to guide you in your connections. This could be either a few notes or a whole piece of music. When you see the word 'lightning', for example, you may start hearing the song 'Greased lightning' from the film of the musical *Grease* and see an image of John Travolta dancing around the car.

Dust	Piano	Bicycle	River	Jamie
Doll	Fly	Busted	Diamonds	Happy
Lamp post	Rocket	Stick	Big	World
Jail	Riot	Moon	Girl	Smile

Cover the words above and finish the words below, writing down the piece of music or the notes you associated to it.

Word	Music	Word	Music
Do_ _		Roc_ _ _	
Bic_ _ _ _ _		Du_ _	
Riv_ _		Sm_ _ _	
Pi_ _ _		Ha_ _ _	
Bus_ _ _		Bi_	
Jam_ _		Mo_ _	
Gi_ _		Ja_ _	
F_ _		La_ _ _ _ _	
St_ _ _		Dia_ _ _ _ _	
Wo_ _ _		Ri_ _	

In what way did this change or improve your connections? Make notes in the space below.

→ I got rhythm

Back in 1997 I was in a show called *Tap Dogs*. There was one routine where we had to remember some complex rhythms and dance them out, using a machine they called a grinder. The grinding on metal caused a 'grzzzz' sound and a large spark through the air, all while we were tap dancing. For some reason, after being shown the routine, I just couldn't get my rhythm right, which meant that everything kept dropping out of synch. I decided that I needed to accelerate my learning process.

I used a simple memory network – the body system – and combined it with the number system, which allowed me to remember what count the 'grzzzz' was on. I remember a big Mac (37) on my knees – 'grzzzz' on the third and seventh count. With this method, it didn't take long before my body got used to the rhythm and I was able to remember the specific points without needing to refer to my images. This idea of picturing and number images is what accelerated my ability to memorize the routine.

 Exercise 65

TAPPING IT OUT

Clap out the following ten rows of eight counts at a steady rhythm, emphasizing the counts in bold by clapping more loudly. Use creative memorization to help you learn the routine by heart.

- ▶ 1, 2, 3, **4**, 5, 6, **7**, 8 (tip: RaKe)
- ▶ 1, **2**, 3, 4, 5, **6**, 7, 8
- ▶ 1, 2, **3**, 4, 5, 6, **7**, 8
- ▶ 1, **2**, 3, 4, 5, **6**, 7, **8**
- ▶ 1, 2, 3, **4**, 5, **6**, 7, 8
- ▶ 1, 2, **3**, 4, 5, 6, **7**, 8
- ▶ 1, 2, 3, **4**, 5, 6, **7**, 8
- ▶ 1, 2, 3, **4**, 5, 6, **7**, 8
- ▶ 1, **2**, 3, 4, **5**, 6, 7, 8
- ▶ 1, 2, 3, 4, 5, 6, 7, **8**

Cover the numbers and clap out the correct rhythm.

→ Music for movement

When you are learning a sequence of physical movements, music can be a terrific tool for helping you get the sequence into your body. If you have ever danced or done an activity like yoga, you may have experienced this. The music guides you along so that, when you hear a particular section of the music, it helps to trigger or remind you of the movement.

Exercise 66

MUSICAL MOVES

Think about any activity you have in your life that involves you performing a sequence of movements, such as dancing, aerobics, martial arts, Pilates or yoga.

Try the following:

- ▶ **Pick** a piece of music.
- ▶ **Storyboard** a sequence of movements.
- ▶ Play the music and use your storyboard to **imagine** doing each movement at a different point in the music.
- ▶ Play the music while doing the sequence, looking at your storyboard and **feeling** where the movements correspond to a specific point in the music.
- ▶ **Rehearse** the whole sequence mentally.
- ▶ **Do** the full sequence without the music.

Use the box below to create your storyboard.

→ Memory lane

You already know that music can trigger memories; this is a useful skill if you are searching your memory banks. With this knowledge, you can use music as another way of expanding your memory networks, building your capability to remember more information.

MAPPING MUSIC NETWORKS

This exercise aims to spark off more ideas for memory networks. It involves creating a new mind map, similar to the one you created in Exercise 33.

This time, use different pieces of music to let your mind wander and feed back ideas on experiences from your life, from which you can create a memory network.

▶ Choose three separate music tracks you enjoy or put your music player on shuffle and use the first three that come up. Let the pieces spark happy memories of events. Capture these experiences and see how many memory networks you can start to create.

▶ For the purpose of this activity, create just ten files for each network, which should be enough to give you a good sense of where you are, so that you can come back to them later and extend them.

Use the box below to create your mind map.

→ Your musical iMind

Have you ever been in a conversation where you have tried to remember the name of an artist or a piece of music? You hear it in your head but you can't seem to access any information on it. Have you ever felt 'left out' because everyone else seemed clued in to a particular piece of music or artist? Perhaps you are the complete opposite and you remember everything about all your favourite artists and their music.

Whichever side you live on, knowing more about the music you like can be a satisfying experience. The following offers a strategy to build up a set of personal playlists, so that you can call on them at the appropriate time.

You could think of this as your iMind music library, similar to a mental version of iTunes, containing all your favourite tracks. You hear some music that triggers your internal playlists (a memory network) that provide relevant information (artist and track, etc.), which you can then project on to your iMind to talk about.

MEMORIZING PLAYLISTS

To get you started, here is a list of well-known tracks with a few key details. Listen to each track and let it inspire some imagery that connects it to an image of the artist and the date. Practise recreating the images and hearing a snippet of the track in your mind.

Artist	Track	Year	Reference story
Queen	Bohemian Rhapsody	1975	
John Lennon	Imagine	1980	
Robbie Williams	Angels	1997	
Beatles	Hey Jude	1968	
Nirvana	Smells Like Teen Spirit	1991	
Oasis	Live Forever	1994	
Oasis	Wonderwall	1995	

Artist	Track	Year	Reference story
U2	One	1992	
Verve	Bitter-sweet Symphony	1997	
U2	With or Without You	1987	
Beatles	Penny Lane/Strawberry Fields Forever	1967	
Beach Boys	Good Vibrations	1966	
REM	Losing my Religion	1991	
Bob Dylan	Like a Rolling Stone	1965	
Beach Boys	God Only Knows	1966	
REM	Everybody Hurts	1993	
Kinks	Waterloo Sunset	1967	
Oasis	Don't Look Back in Anger	1996	
Procol Harum	A Whiter Shade of Pale	1967	
Led Zeppelin	Stairway To Heaven	1971	

Now take this quiz to test your memorization.

→ In 1965, which artist had a hit with 'Like A Rolling Stone'?

_____

→ In which year was Queen's classic 'Bohemian Rhapsody' released?

_____

→ Which Robbie Williams classic was released in 1997?

_____

→ Which two Beach Boys songs feature in this list?

_____

→ 'Strawberry Fields' was a hit for the Beatles in 1967 along with what other track?

_____

→ Oasis released 'Wonderwall' in which year?

_____

→ 'Losing my Religion' and 'Everybody Hurts' were hits for which band?

_____

→ Procol Harum released which song in 1967?

_____

→ John Lennon's 'Imagine' was released in which year?

_____

→ Which song did Nirvana release in 1991?

_____

··

→ Tag it!

You may have been in a situation where you hear a great new music track on the car radio or from the sound system in a shop. You want to remember it for later so that you can search for it, get it on iTunes or buy a physical copy, but you don't have any way of writing it down. If you are into nextGen apps you may have tried something like Shazam, but if you are driving you still have a problem. However, with your current skill-set this is a fairly easy memory to create, as the following exercise shows.

There are several ways you could approach this problem. Think about what your approach might be.

REMEMBERING THE TOP TRACKS

Adapt this exercise to suit your style. It shows a way to design a small temporary memory network that you can use as a 'net' to hold information relating to your track for a short period of time, before moving the tracks over to a more permanent memory network later.

You can use this memory network over and over again for the simple process of tagging and remembering new tracks that you hear.

- ▶ Create a memory network with just ten files.
- ▶ Imagine that you heard each of the following tracks on the radio while out and about or in a car.
- ▶ Create an image for the name of the track and associate it to a file.
- ▶ Test this out by running through all ten images and checking that the snippet of music is triggered.

The above should be enough to spark off who the artist is. If you need an image for the artist, add this too.

Artist	Single	Date, 2013
will.i.am featuring Britney Spears	Scream & Shout	13 January
Bingo Players featuring Far East Movement	Get Up (Rattle)	27 January
Macklemore & Ryan Lewis featuring Wanz	Thrift Shop	10 February
Avicii vs. Nicky Romero	I Could Be the One	17 February
One Direction	One Way or Another (Teenage Kicks)	24 February
Justin Timberlake	Mirrors	3 March
The Saturdays featuring Sean Paul	What About Us	24 March
PJ & Duncan	Let's Get Ready to Rhumble	31 March

Summary

In this chapter you looked at how music can be used to bring episodic memories back to you, opening up your mind to new ideas for memory networks. You practised heightening your ability to identify instruments in a piece of music and looking at what type of music certain words inspire. When you saw diamonds, did you think 'Lucy in the Sky with Diamonds' or 'Diamonds are a Girl's Best Friend', or something else?

As well as using music as an aid to remembering physical sequences, you explored how to remember rhythms through using visual imagery. You built up your personal playlists by adding more knowledge around your favourite tracks and created a simple strategy to remember tracks any time, anywhere.

To continue building your memory for music, seek out opportunities to remember your favourite music and look for ways in which you can incorporate music and rhythm into your learning.

What I have learned

 What are my thoughts, feelings and insights on what I have read so far?

_____

_____

_____

Use the space below to summarize the actions to take as a result of reading this chapter.

_____

_____

_____

_____

Where to next?

In the next chapter we are going to review the area of memory for picture smarts. How can we use visual and spatial pictures to be more effective at taking notes, solving problems and making information memorable?

9

Memory for picture smarts

In this chapter you will learn:

▶ how to increase your visualization skills
▶ to make any type of information memorable
▶ to recall details when you most need them
▶ how to remember directions
▶ how to remember where you left things!

As mentioned at the beginning of Chapter 4 on memory strategies, the Ancient Greek poet Simonides of Ceos noticed that he was still able to recall where people had been sitting around the banquet table after they had been buried in rubble. This led him to realize that our ability to remember where things are visually in space is extremely efficient.

This chapter will tap into your innate visual and spatial memory capabilities. Using these natural abilities, you can improve your observational skills, your memory for directions and your ability to reflect your ideas in the form of symbols, sketches, drawings or maps. You will also be able to extend your visual expertise to remembering directions and programming your memory for the future.

'A picture is a poem without words.'

Horace

MAPPING YOUR VISUAL MEMORY

How can being smarter with your recall of pictures benefit you in your life? As with the previous chapters, think of someone you regard as having an excellent visual memory. On a scale of 1 to 10, if they are a 10, where are you in terms of:

- ▶ your current ability?
- ▶ your potential?
- ▶ your goal in three months' time?

Mark the point where you think you are in terms of your visual recall on the scale below.

1_____10

Think about what it would mean to be smarter with pictures.

→ What would happen if you could increase your performance by 10–50 per cent?

_____

→ How would this make you feel?

_____

→ What current challenges do you face?

_____

Give yourself five minutes to create your thoughts, this time using some form of visual note-taking in the space below. This could be pictures, mind mapping or storyboards, etc. Make sure you play back verbally what you write down.

→ Visual thinking

How well can you draw? Do you get excited at the thought of it? Is it something you do well or does it feel like child's play?

Children are interesting in terms of drawing. While I was writing this chapter, my five-year-old showed me this picture. What do you think it means?

Look at the picture as you read the following the story, which is how Elijah described his picture in his own words. Reference each part he is talking about.

'These are his powers, he shot them altogether and it made a mega explosion. He's got an X cape, because these bits are X Frisbees and all of these are spiky, 'cause it's all superhero frisbees that comes out of his body. He's wearing normal clothes, except superhero clothes! How many superheros do you know that wear normal superhero clothes? The squiggle is his air power, he's got one big bit of air power, so it will explode any minute now.'

Look at the picture again and write down in the space below what you remember about Elijah's pictures, in your own words.

How much of what you captured above mirrors Elijah's explanation? My guess is that, while your language will have been more sophisticated, you will more than likely have pulled out similar points.

For Elijah, there is no stigma attached to drawing. He uses it to express himself in order to convey a message, one that makes sense to him and is memorable. Let's say you are worried that you 'can't draw'. What would happen if you started to think like a child again? Rather than focusing on whether something is good or bad, what if you just had some fun expressing your ideas and thoughts in a way that was more symbolic?

With a few simple shapes (square, circle, triangle, line, dots and blobs), you can draw pretty much anything. Squares and circles can create simple cars. Other symbols, such as icons, connectors and 3D text, can be used to express your thoughts. Stick figures can show how a person is feeling or reacting in a situation. Simple drawings like these can have a big impact when it comes to solving problems through visual notes, capturing talks or communicating concepts in a way that makes sense.

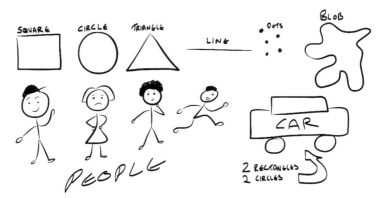

Simple shapes and stick figures can convey ideas effectively

Here's an example of how you could draw the first five elements in the Big Ben story. Accuracy isn't as important as understanding: for example, even if the dinosaur looks like a sausage, *you* know that your image represents the dinosaur.

Elements in the Big Ben story

 ## Exercise 71

DISCOVERING YOUR INNER ARTIST

Recreate your own version of the Big Ben story in the space below, using any of the simple shapes and ideas suggested above. Think like five-year-old Elijah: there is no right or wrong way to approach it – you are simply expressing your ideas.

By using your visual skills, you are instantly creating meaning in concepts and ideas as well as making them memorable. It is also an easy step to use creative memorization to associate your visual notes in your mind.

→ Visual thinking in the real world

Here is an example of visual thinking in the real world. It is an example based on Dan Roam's 'back of a napkin' idea – that you can solve any problem with a simple picture – and it represents my own Myers-Briggs Type. The Myers-Briggs Type Indicator (MBTI) process aims to give a person a deeper understanding of their natural preferences. Developed by Katherine Briggs and her daughter Isabel Myers, it was inspired by Carl Jung's theories of psychological types.

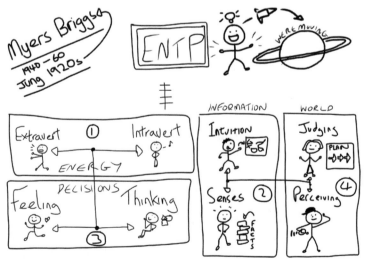

Visual notes for an MBTI

While Myers-Briggs is outside the scope of this book, this visual note starts to give you a sense of what it might mean for you.

▶ Is your energy directed outwards (extravert) or inwards (introvert)?

▶ Do you take in information by intuition, seeing patterns and making connections, or do you look for hard sensory information in terms of facts?

▶ Once you have your information, do you make your decisions through feelings or logical thinking?

▶ How do you deal with the world around you? Are you the type of person who always knows the plan, or are you fuelled by working at the last minute?

While the Myers-Briggs Type Indicator doesn't seek to put a person in a 'box', it does give an indication of a person's most natural tendencies. While we are all probably capable of doing any of the above to a high standard, we may have preferences: in the same way that we may prefer to write with our right hand as opposed to our left, with practice we could probably become proficient at both.

USING VISUAL THINKING

Think of a topic that you know well, perhaps relating to your role at work. Spend just ten minutes sketching out this topic in the space below, in a way that will make it easy to understand, memorable and fun! Then share it with a friend.

→ Mind mapping

At the beginning of this book you were introduced to a high-level view of how to mind map. As a whole-brain tool, mind maps are beneficial in at least four key areas:

- ▶ creating (new ideas, problem solving)
- ▶ capturing (taking away the big ideas)
- ▶ consuming (understanding and remembering)
- ▶ communicating (displaying structure in an organic memorable way).

Although people have always made visual notes and diagrams, Tony Buzan developed the idea further with his mind maps™ back in the 1960s. Here is a mind map capturing the main concepts of mind mapping.

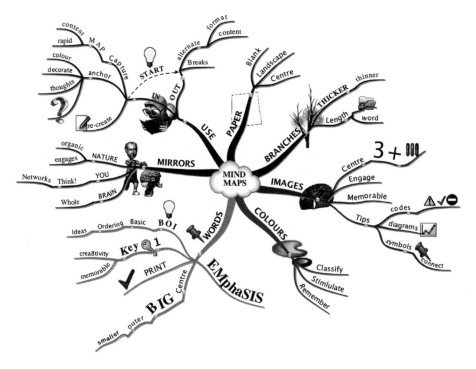

The concepts of mind mapping shown in ThinkBuzan's iMindMap

Words	Branches	Images	Colours
Only one word per branch; use size for EmPHasis!	Reflect your personal style; limit the branch length to that of the word or image. Use connector branches to associate other branches in close vicinity.	Images everywhere! Use dimension to engage, icons to draw attention and symbols to connect similar ideas on opposite sides of a mind map.	Use colours to classify, reflect emotion and draw attention.

Think about how mind maps could relate to the learning cycle. Your sensory inputs might be:

▶ visual – as you create

▶ auditory – as you hone your thoughts

▶ kinaesthetic – as you draw and spark off emotion

▶ potentially even gustatory and olfactory – as you map out a tasty chocolate gateau with fresh cream recipe!

What about integration? This is when you reflect on what you already know, abstract your own thoughts, view the big picture, and then zoom into the detail. How might you use a mind map to test out your ideas and take action?

▶ Will you use it to talk through an issue with someone?

▶ Will you use its branches to remember key areas for an exam?

▶ Will you use it to solve a problem that feels too big?

As you think about the process of mind mapping, it becomes clear how synergetic it is with the learning cycle and the brain's optimum patterns for learning.

 Exercise 73

PITCHING WITH A MIND MAP

Use your visual note taking to create a mind map of a 20-minute presentation for a game show, based on a topic that you are passionate about. Imagine that you are going to walk into a room with five people and pitch this idea, using your mind map as a visual guide.

Create your mind map below:

▶ **Start with your central image and some main branches.**

▶ **Alternate between content (the words) and format (the colours, icons, symbols, images, frames and connectors).**

▶ **Keep the flow of the mind map going.**

▶ **Take no more than 15 minutes to map out your whole 20-minute presentation.**

Imagine that, with two minutes to go before you start your presentation, there has been a last-minute change. Rather than having 20 minutes to present to five people, you only have 60 seconds to pitch your idea to the head of the company. Grab a partner, friend or just pitch out loud your 20-minute idea in 60 seconds, using your mind map to get across the essence of your idea.

→ Remembering directions

Have you ever been in a situation, either on foot or in a car, where you have had to ask someone for directions? Do you listen intently, only to glaze over before they are halfway through giving you the information? Or do you immediately understand exactly how to get where you want to go and lock a mental map in your mind?

When trying to remember a set of directions, you can take various approaches using creative memorization.

▶ First, decide whether to create visualizations internally or externally on your iMind.

▶ Are you going to use a visual code: rats for right, leaves for left, etc?

▶ Might you use a journey you know well and simply associate the visual codes to it?

▶ Are you going to create the journey purely in your imagination, highlighting the main points, creating the journey in your mind, exaggerating the landmarks where you need to take an action, memorizing in the same way that you would when creating a new memory network?

Let's look at an example with two different approaches; there will be others you can come up with.

DESTINATION: BUTCHER'S SHOP

'Take the first turning on the left, continue to the end of the road, turn left, and the butcher is on the right.'

Option 1: Use a visual code and a memory network of your own choosing (you will need four files). The code here is left = leaf, right = rat, end of road = end sign.

Imagine:

▶ File no.1: a leaf (first left)

▶ File no. 2: end sign (end of road)

▶ File no. 3: a leaf (next left)

▶ File no. 4: a butcher's filled with rats (butcher's on right).

Option 2: Use your iMind to project the journey visually out in front of you, seeing each direction as it happens, exaggerating the main points and reciting aloud. Think of this in the same way you would if you were creating a new memory network. All you actually have to remember here are four locations on an 'imagined' memory network.

1 You see yourself driving ahead and taking the first turning on the left. Pick a specific point on this imagined journey and say 'Number 1.' See yourself turning left, imagine what it feels like and say it out loud.

2 See yourself driving to the end of the road and say 'Number 2.' Then do the same as in point 1 above.

3 See location no. 3 on your left (perhaps a tree) and say 'Number 3.'

4 See the butcher on your right and say "Number 4.'

With this option you can choose to get your physicality involved, using your hands as if you were directing yourself along the journey.

HOW DO I GET TO...?

Here are five sets of directions to memorize. Choose one of the methods already described to memorize each set of directions, or create your own method that plays to your strengths. Each journey is progressively more complicated.

You should aim to file each of these sets of directions on a memory network, to answer the questions that follow. A suggestion here is to associate the destination to each file.

▶ Use creative memorization to engage your visual, spatial skills.
▶ Make sure you have understood the directions by summarizing them back (this has the added benefit of using your short-term memory and phonological loop in order to understand what has been said).

Destination	Directions
The butcher's shop	Take the first turning on the left, continue to the end of the road, turn left and the butcher is on the right.
Number 10	Go straight over the first set of traffic lights, turn right at the second set of traffic lights, follow the road around the bend and take the second turning on the left after the post office to get to number 10.
The restaurant via the chemist's	Turn left out of the doctor's surgery, go to the end of the road and turn right, then take the second on the left and the chemist is on the left-hand side next to the baker's. Then go left out of the driveway, right and right again, straight over the roundabout and the entrance to the restaurant is on the right.
The motorway	Follow the road to the roundabout where you take the first exit, go under the railway bridge and continue on this road until you pass the library on your left. Then take the first turning on the right. Continue up the hill, turn right at the top, carry on past the park, take the first right, right again and then carry on along the road until you reach a T-junction. Turn left and take the first right at the next roundabout, at the traffic lights turn right, follow the road on to the dual carriageway, pull into the right-hand lane, follow the signs for the M25 and at the junction turn right on to the motorway slip road.
The swimming pool via the school	Go straight over the traffic lights, then take the second exit from the mini roundabout, follow the road and continue straight through two sets of traffic lights and then take the next left, then second right and pull into the school on the left. Turn left out of the school and at the roundabout take the first exit and join the dual carriageway. Take the third exit from the carriageway and at the roundabout take the first exit. Follow the road and at the next roundabout take the fourth exit, then the second turning on the right, over the T-junction with a hotel on the right-hand side. Leave the M25 at junction 15 and join the M4, exit the M4 at junction 12, take the third exit from the roundabout, follow the road, at the first set of traffic lights turn left, take the second turning on the left and the swimming pool is on the left-hand side.

Test your recall

Imagine you are giving directions to someone who is lost. How would you tell them how to get to the following destinations?

→ The butcher's shop?

_____

_____

_____

→ Number 10?

_____

_____

_____

→ The restaurant via the chemist's?

_____

_____

_____

_____

→ The motorway?

_____

_____

_____

_____

_____

→ The swimming pool via the school?

_____

_____

_____

_____

_____

_____

_____

_____

_____

→ Information through the brain

We are constantly receiving a variety of information from the external world via our senses. As we watch a presentation, for example, and see the slides, hear the lecturer speaking and sense the too-warm room through our skin and perhaps our nose, all this information is being sifted through to the reticular activating system (RAS), which resides in the brainstem. The RAS is permanently turned on, and it sends the information to the brain's central relay system, the thalamus, for sorting.

The thalamus will decide what it needs to do next and send the information to the appropriate part of the cerebral cortex (visual, auditory, etc.), where it can be acted upon or stored in the memory. If it is the latter, then information is relayed from the cortex to the hippocampus, which catalogues and files it. If the information has emotional content, it is sent to the amygdala for a similar procedure.

BRAIN FLOW

Think about how you might represent the flow of information through your brain in a visual, compelling and memorable manner.

Capture your approach in the space below, memorize it and then recite it aloud.

→ # Tags and triggers

One of the statements often heard from a person talking about improving their memory is they can never find their keys or wallet. Since this happens to most of us at one time or another, it is more of an inconvenience than a real driver to improve memory. On the other hand, when it does happen, it can be very frustrating, especially if you are a busy person with a lot going on.

Think about whether any of the strategies or techniques you have learned so far would equip you to remember where you put your keys or wallet.

Exercise 76

USING MEMORY TAGS

A memory tag is a simple technique that will let you remember where you left an item you put down somewhere – whether it's at home, at work or while you are out and about. For this activity to work on an ongoing basis, you need to condition it into your body so that it happens without you consciously thinking about it. It is a fairly simple concept and, if you work with it over the course of a week, you will find that it will work more and more often, and you'll find things much more easily. This will be partly because you have given it your focus.

Follow this simple process:

▶ Create a tag word or phrase – something like 'Tag it!' can work quite well – that is personal to you.

▶ Craft a specific physical action to go with this tag word, in the same way that a magician may wave their hand in a specific movement when they do a trick. You may find it works well to touch the item as you do the movement. This distinctive movement will help focus your attention.

▶ Create a simple association: as you lay down your keys on the table, for example, say 'Tag it!' while doing your action and visualize the keys falling through the table top or getting tied to the table with chains. You will most likely build up a small selection of methods to tag your items.

▶ Later, when you think about where you left your keys, this will trigger the most recent memory tag.

→ In order to test this out, choose three to five items that you use frequently (wallet, keys, phone, etc.). Write them down here.

_____

_____

Over the next seven days, practise tagging. While you may not get a 'direct hit' every time, you will find that your accuracy increases and memory tagging becomes less conscious and more subconscious.

While an ability to remember where you put things can be useful, perhaps a more rewarding skill is being able to programme yourself to remember to do certain actions at a specific point in the future. This could be paying money into the bank, calling a client or buying the milk. By creating a 'future memory' in a location where you know you will be at a certain time, you can set yourself up to take a required action. This programming essentially conditions your brain to respond to a specific stimulus, your subconscious notifying your conscious that it should act.

Exercise 77

CREATING MEMORY TRIGGERS

This exercise aims to enable you to remember to carry out tasks on your to-do list by using memory triggers.

Think of something you need to do later (such as buy milk) and create a future memory, as follows:

▶ Imagine what time it is when you will be carrying out the task.
▶ See the event in your mind's eye: for example, as you walk past the newsagent, you see a gigantic bottle of milk jump out of the shop and say, 'Buy me!'
▶ Make a physical action as you see this happening and say a trigger word. You might, for example, see the images, click your fingers and say the word 'alert'.

Start by trying one or two of these triggers a day. In order for them to work, you need to exaggerate your 'future memory' triggers. If your alert goes off a bit before you get to the newsagent – or whatever the location is where you will carry out the task – be sure to remember and act upon it when you get there.

Try testing this out over the next seven days. With practice, you should be able to set up effective future memories for your daily to-do list that will trigger the action needed.

Summary

In this chapter you have tapped into your inner artist and constructed skills around various forms of visual thinking. This has the impact of turning complex ideas into something simpler to understand, more engaging and more memorable. Look for ways to put these skills into practice in your day-to-day life.

Before moving on, to go back to Exercise 70 and update the scale with where you believe you are now.

What I have learned

What are my thoughts, feelings and insights on what I have read so far?

_____

_____

_____

Use the space below to summarize the actions to take as a result of reading this chapter.

_____

_____

_____

_____

Where to next?

In the next chapter we are going to be looking at how to improve your memory for movement, or 'body smarts', and what strategies we can use to learn new physical skills.

10 Memory for body smarts

In this chapter you will learn:
- ▶ how to increase your ability to learn movement through motivation
- ▶ ways to use metaphor to increase understanding in your body
- ▶ to increase your knowledge of movement and get it 'into your body'
- ▶ to employ visual cues to memorize sequences
- ▶ how to use memory triggers to look after your posture.

Do you learn by physically doing things? This chapter will look at how you can use your kinaesthetic abilities – your 'body smarts' – to help your memory and at how to bring creative memorization into play to improve your performance in physical activities.

As with other skills such as drawing, it is easy for people to label themselves and say things like, 'I'm no good at sports' or 'I just can't dance'. While this may seem true from their experience – and while it will not be their natural preference – like any other type of intelligence, kinaesthetic ability can be improved. A person who doesn't do sports can be excellent at a physical activity like playing the piano or touch-typing on a laptop, both of which require a high level of co-ordination.

"'Tis the mind that makes the body rich.'

William Shakespeare

Exercise 78

MAPPING YOUR PHYSICAL ABILITY

Here is your regular diagnostic activity. Think of a person whom you regard as having excellent physical ability. On a scale of 1 to 10, if they are a 10, where are you in terms of:

▶ your current ability?

▶ your potential?

▶ your goal for three months' time?

Mark the point where you rate your physical ability on the scale below.

1_____10

What would it mean to you to be smarter with your body?

→ What would happen if you could increase your performance by 10–50 per cent?

_____

→ How would this make you feel?

_____

→ What current challenges do you face?

_____

Using your notes, give yourself five minutes to elaborate on your thoughts in the space opposite. Since you now have experience with both visual note taking and mind mapping, opt for either of these for this activity. Make sure you still play back verbally what you write down.

→ Rewards

Thinking back to childhood memories of running cross-country on a Sunday afternoon training session with my dad in Aberdeen, I remember a particular occasion where the wind was almost gale force and wondering why we had to train in such weather. Halfway through the session I felt like giving up. However, although the idea of being disappointed in myself didn't sit well, a stronger motivator for carrying on was the praise I would get from my dad when I finished and the longer-term goal of doing well in a race I had been training for all year. A thought similar to, 'Well, if I can finish this I can probably finish anything' crossed my mind. This filled me with self-satisfaction and a feeling of determination that boosted me on and renewed my motivation. Looking back, I understand the lesson my dad was sharing with me that day.

To increase your physical intelligence, you could hypothesize that somewhere inside you there has to be a strong level of motivation, a driving factor that compels you to move forward. Thinking about what it might cost you if you don't take some action can be a great kick-start in the short term. However, the classic, 'I need to get fit after Christmas, since I've put on half my body weight in turkey!' that most of us have experienced, tends not to be long lasting.

Reward, on the other hand, specifically the emotion that comes with that reward, can help in the short term and also in supporting long-term motivation, especially if it is associated to our core values (health, happiness, making a difference, family, etc). If a person has a core value of significance to them, such as health, getting a faster running time could be a short-term motivator. If they also have a core value of family, a long-term reward could be keeping fit enough to play with their children as they grow. These values and motivators are, of course, personal to each of us.

Creative memorization can play a part in helping you think up short-term rewards and long-term future memories, generating momentum that pulls you forward. Think back to the effective memory activities in Chapter 3 (on creative memorization) and the emotion that was generated by focusing on a simple object and putting you in a scene at some point in the future.

TARGETS AND REWARDS

Think about a physical activity that you either want to improve or have been putting off doing. This might be anything from a team sport, a martial art or going to the gym, to Pilates, yoga, qigong, dance, t'ai chi, running or swimming.

▶ **What is the short-term cost of not doing it?**

▶ **What short-term reward can you offer yourself for doing it today?**

▶ **What is the long-term future memory you can create that is connected to one of your core values? (Think of health, happiness, recognition, security, family, love or something else…)**

Use your visual thinking skills and sketch out the scene below. Then use your affective memory skills to transport yourself there in your mind and experience the emotion that goes along with it.

→ Explicit and implicit learning

Think back to when you first learned a particular sport – perhaps golf, tennis, badminton, netball or something else. You probably had some type of verbal instruction. If you learned to dive, for example, you would have received a procedural set of instructions, such as:

▶ 'Bend down so that your chest is touching the top of your thighs.'

▶ 'Push forward with your arms and legs at the same time.'

▶ 'Straighten your arms above your head and tuck your head in.'

▶ 'Straighten your body once you enter the water and kick.'

While it would have been useful for you to understand the component parts of diving, it is a lot of information to process and think about while you are diving into the water. Most likely you could verbalize what you are 'supposed' to do, although it does not immediately correlate that you will be able to perform these actions in your body. You can think of this as **explicit learning**, where a series of detailed instructions is given. However, not only does it take time to assimilate these instructions into your body but there is also the chance of increased stress as you 'try to get it right' and you experience 'paralysis by analysis' (Masters, 1992).

Implicit learning occurs where the learner is given no explicit verbal instruction but still acquires the skills necessary to perform the action. An example of this might be to use metaphor. Before you dive, rather than being given a set of steps to follow as in the example above, you are asked to imagine that you are a 'recoiled arrow ready to be fired from a crossbow, and when you pull the trigger you shoot yourself into the water'. What do you think your body would do?

While you may not execute the perfect dive straight away, by focusing on this image as you take action you will no doubt push forward with your arms and legs at the same time, straighten your arms above your head, tuck your head in and straighten your body, all with a good amount of energy and force. You can then make small adjustments as you begin to perfect your dive. Since there is less analysis, there is also less chance of choking under pressure. The act of diving is also easier to remember as you have chunked up the process into one simple image.

Combining these two methods of learning with setting reward targets will keep your mind motivated and away from over-thinking, assisting you in achieving that state of flow.

Ideally, aim for a good balance between explicit and implicit methods of learning a physical skill. Understand the instructions intellectually and then let your brian step out of the way so that your body can go ahead and do it! This is where metaphor or analogy can play its part.

METAPHOR MOVES

In this exercise you will create a metaphor or analogy that will help you perform a physical activity implicitly.

Think of an activity that you currently perform or would like to perform in the future. Perhaps it is an activity you find a challenge or that you tend to over-think. An example is in Pilates, where you are lying on your back, knees pointing to the ceiling and feet on the floor.

▶ Explicit instruction using a technical step-by-step approach: 'Engage your pelvic floor muscles and transversus abdominis.' This is an accurate procedural description and intellectually it creates domain knowledge.

▶ Implicit instruction using metaphor: 'Zip up your core' or 'Use the light in your centre and have it gently drop into the floor.' Even if you have no idea what or where your pelvic floor and transversus abdominis muscles are, you will have an idea of how to perform this movement.

Design your metaphor, making your notes in the box below.

→ Acting out

It may not always be necessary to be able to explain the physical actions you perform. If however, you are an instructor, coach or teacher, understanding information about your domain is indispensable. This idea of getting words 'into your body' is also an essential skill for actors. When performing in a scene, the last thing you want to be doing is 'thinking' about what to say next; you are waiting to react.

In Exercise 46, Business terms, and Exercise 47, Learning another language, you explored how to make terminology and words more memorable. In the following exercise you are going to take a similar approach, adding a physical element that will help you 'hook up' the meaning of the word into your body.

ABSORBING ANATOMY TERMS

In this activity you are going to absorb a number of anatomy terms into your body. In order to do this, you are going to need to get physical and use your iMind:

1 Create an image for the key word.
2 Project it externally using your iMind.
3 Physically act out what the word represents.

Here are some examples.

▶ For Transverse Plane, imagine a train driving around your waist, while you stand up taking your hand across your waist as you divide your body in half (upper and lower parts).
▶ For Superior, imagine you are Superman as you look up, throwing your arms closer to your head as if you are about to take off.
▶ For Distal, imagine a Distilled bottle hovering away from the trunk of your body as you reach out to grab it.

Rather than write out the following terms as reference stories, simply read each one and follow steps 1–3 above.

Planes of movement	Definition
Median (sagittal) plane	Divides the body into left and right halves
Frontal (or coronal) plane	Divides the body into front and back portions
Transverse plane	Divides the body into upper and lower parts
Directions and positions	
Superior	Closer to the head
Inferior	Closer to the feet
Posterior	Farther towards the back of the body than another structure
Anterior	Refers to a structure farther in front
Medial	A structure closer to the midline (or centre) of the body
Lateral	A structure farther away from the midline
Distal	A structure farther away from the trunk or the body's midline
Proximal	A structure closer to the trunk
Superficial	A structure closer to the body's surface
Deep	A structure deeper in the body

→ Movement!

In Exercise 27, Using your iMind, you were introduced to the idea of visual cues. In Exercise 48, Storyboards, you learned how to create a set of visual cues in order to remember a presentation. Those cues appeared on your iMind, projected out there in front of you, acting almost like an autocue system guiding you to what was next. In a physical activity, a visual cue could be a picture that represents a set of movements.

▶ In **tap dancing**, once you have mastered the steps – shuffles, beats, pull-backs, wings, and so on – you can use visual cues to represent a whole sequence. Each of these cues lets you know what the next sequence is, guiding you through the entire routine.

▶ In the form of **Wing Chun kung fu** called Sil Lum Tao (Little Idea), you go through a sequence of movements, again in order to accelerate getting the sequence into your body. You may create a set of visual cues to represent the movements – opening stance, drawing the centre line, three prayers, etc.

▶ In **Pilates,** you might need to remember that a roll-up came after a cat stretch, so you picture a cat and associate it to a jam roll, sequencing the visual cues in your mind.

VISUAL CUES

This exercise is similar to Exercise 66, Musical moves, but this time with the addition of a set of visual cues. This activity should be as simple as taking your current storyboard, bringing its images to life, connecting them together and projecting them on your iMind as a set of visual cues.

Here is a reminder of the steps in Exercise 66 with the visual cues added:

▶ **Pick** a piece of music.

▶ **Storyboard** a sequence of movements.

▶ Play the music and use your storyboard to **imagine** doing each movement at a different point in the music.

▶ Play the music doing the sequence, looking at your storyboard and **feeling** where the movements correspond to a specific place in the music.

▶ Create **visual cues** (essentially linking items in your storyboard together).

▶ **Rehearse** the whole sequence mentally.

▶ **Do** the full sequence without the music.

Test your recall by running through your activity, using your visual cues as a guide!

SEQUENCING

Before you begin learning a new physical activity, you can prepare for it by creating a sequence of visual cues. This process of sequencing can offer you a head start.

For example, you could use creative memorization to turn each of the following ten yoga, qigong and Pilates exercises into a visual cue, construct a chain for each one, project them onto your iMind and recite each exercise aloud. If you were to then go to a class, you would be already primed to learn the physical movement.

Create three sequences of visual cues for the following exercises.

Yoga exercises	Qigong exercises	Pilates exercises
1 Mountain pose	1 The sun	1 Hundred
2 Downward dog	2 Pushing the mountains away	2 Roll up
3 Warrior	3 The water	3 Roll over
4 Tree pose	4 The rock	4 Spine twist
5 Bridge pose	5 Pushing the clouds	5 Teaser
6 Triangle pose	6 The pine tree branch	6 Neck pull
7 Seated twist	7 The turtle	7 Seal
8 Cobra	8 Cloud hands	8 Scissors
9 Child's pose	9 Beautiful woman turns the waist	9 Side kick
10 Crow pose	10 Gazing backwards at the moon	10 Swan

How would you apply this process to a physical activity you want to learn?

_____

_____

_____

_____

_____

_____

→ Tell the story

It is not only big physical movements that can be learned and remembered by combining physical actions with visual cues. You can also memorize smaller-scale actions like keyboard commands and shortcuts.

Since most shortcuts require the command button, there is no need to create an image for it. In the following exercise we can represent the key option by imagining a sticky substance (there is no logical connection here, but since you will only have a few of these it will be very easy to remember).

MEMORIZING KEYBOARD SHORTCUTS

This exercise uses some iTunes keyboard shortcuts for a Mac. For each shortcut you can act out a small story that not only gets the movement into your body but also links up the meaning.

Here are some examples:

▶ Imagine you are in space and you press play. While seeing this image, you do the physical action of pressing space.

▶ Imagine a sticky substance (option) mutes your speakers as an arrow is fired into it. See this image and press option + command + ↓.

Go ahead and create your own reference stories. As always, there is no need to write them down unless you feel it helps you clarify or accelerate the process. With practice you will just do these in your head.

Command	Show visualizer	Reference story
Space	Play and pause	
Command + .	Stop	
Option + Command + →	Move forward in track	
Command + ,	Open preferences	
Option + Command + ←	Move back in a track	
Option + Command + M	Minimize or maximise	
Command + ↑	Increase volume	
Command + ↓	Decrease volume	
Option + Command + ↓	Mute and keep playing	
Command + E	Eject disc	

→ Programming

When we think about physical intelligence, 'gross motor' activities like dance, martial arts and so on usually come to mind. However, any sequence of physical actions could also be thought of in this category. Computer programming is an interesting example in this context. It is the 'How do I write that?' problem. You might intellectually understand what something means when you read it, but in order to create your own program you have to be able to 'write it out'.

Look at the following javascript function. Think about how you might use visual cues and physical actions to remember it.

function costa(milk,sugar,coffee)

{

var totalCost = (milk+sugar+coffee);

return totalCost;

}

'A JavaScript function is a "recipe" of instructions (i.e. statements or commands) whose purpose is to accomplish a well-defined task. A function's input is called its parameters; its output is called the return value.'

http://sharkysoft.com/tutorials/jsa/content/039.html

1 The first line of code, **function costa(milk,sugar,coffee)**, is saying there will be a function called **costa** and it will ask for three ingredients (parameters **milk,sugar,coffee**).

2 Everything inside the curly brackets { } describes how it will use these three parameters and what the output will be.

3 The second line, **var totalCost = (milk+sugar+coffee)**, is saying there is a variable (a container) called **totalCost** which will add together the totals of milk+sugar+coffee in order to find out the total cost.

4 The last line, **return totalCost,** will return the result.

This function now becomes reusable. To call this function, you could write:

var marksCoffee = costa(20,5,150);

document.write(marksCoffee);

Which would add (20+5+150), giving the total cost of Mark's coffee as 175 or £1.75. To reuse this to work out Sally's large coffee, I might say:

var sallysCoffee = totalCost(20,5,170);

document.write(sallysCoffee);

This would return a result of 195 or £1.95.

If you wanted to try this out in a web page, you could open up a new text file using something like Notepad. Save it as a **coffee-function.html** and type out the following code (this contains some extra html tags):

```
<!DOCTYPE html>

<html>

<body>

<script>

function costa(milk,sugar,coffee)

{

var totalCost = (milk+sugar+coffee);

return totalCost;

}

var marksCoffee = costa(20,5,150);

document.write(marksCoffee);

</script>

</body>

</html>
```

Initially you just want to remember how to 'write the function' so, rather than having to constantly refer to a book, you can picture it in your mind and write it out on a laptop or on paper. This way your comprehension of what is going on will grow as you start to put it into practice, allowing you to focus on the meaning rather than the syntax, accelerating your understanding of words like parameters, variables, statements and how they fit together.

COFFEE TIME

Use creative memorization to remember 'how to write' this function. This is advanced application of creative memorization. It may feel intricate in the beginning but, once this 'clicks', it can open up a world of possibilities in terms of getting complex information into your body in order to achieve results.

```
function costa(milk,sugar,coffee)

{

var totalCost = (milk+sugar+coffee);

return totalCost;

}
```

Before reading the example below, sketch or write out how you would go about this.

Use your iMind to act out the following.

Story	Purpose
Imagine you have a nice reusable mug.	This is your function.
On the side write what it's for: costa (milk, sugar, coffee).	This is the name of your function and the name of your parameters.
Open the lid.	This is your first curly bracket.
Grab a metal container.	This will always mean variable (var).
Write a name on the container, total Cost.	This is the name of the variable.
Fill up with ingredients = to the top (milk+sugar+coffee).	These are your parameters.
Press a return button on the side of the totalCost container, to mix everything up.	Tell yourself that this button will always mean return followed by the 'name' of the function (costa in this case).
Put the container inside your mug.	It's inside your curly bracket.
Close your lid.	This is your second curly bracket.

Before writing out the function, make sure the story is clear in your mind.

Write the function in the space below, checking your accuracy against the previous page. If you need to, correct any mistakes and write it out again until it feels locked in.

→ Memory and body awareness

Do you ever find that slouching over a computer desk for hours on end causes you backache? Having a better memory will not fix back pain, but you can use some of what you already know to help yourself become more aware of what is happening with your body and take preventive measures.

Exercise 86

SIT UP!

Think about how you might use a memory trigger to pay more attention to your body while working on a PC or laptop.

Here's a simple exercise to help you do this:

1   Sit in front of your keyboard and start typing.

2   Let your body fall into a slouch position and imagine the computer screen opening its eyes, smiling at you, growing arms and lifting you by the shoulders into a better position.

3   While doing this, have it say something to you.

4   Do this five times, making it bigger, funnier and more real each time.

5   Let yourself know that this will happen every time you start to slouch over your keyboard.

Summary

In this chapter you have experienced using implicit learning to make physical activities easier to understand and potentially less stressful when performed. You have also applied creative memorization to the sequencing of movements and used your body to act out the meaning of words. You have carried out more advanced creative memorization to accelerate the rate at which you can put complex information into practice and applied memory triggers to raise awareness of your posture so that you can avoid aches and pains.

You can now look for ways in your daily life to apply what you have practised, making more use of implicit learning, visual cues and physical actions for yourself.

What I have learned

What are my thoughts, feelings and insights on what I have read so far?

_____

_____

_____

Use the space below to summarize the actions to take as a result of reading this chapter.

_____

_____

_____

_____

Where to next?

In the next chapter you will take a journey into the last of the 'memory smarts', your emotional intelligence. You will discover how a better memory can improve your understanding of yourself and how you interact socially.

11 Memory for emotional smarts

Memory is a very personal thing. Although anyone can use the strategies in this workbook, they will not be integrated and applied by everyone in the same way. You may prefer strong visual images, or you may like to describe an image or get a sense of what it feels like. Those images and associations are unique to us as individuals.

Being aware of what works for you as an individual is key to understanding how to put creative memorization into practice and derive real value from it. Unlocking this emotional intelligence within yourself is what will give you the edge as you adapt the strategies in this book into a 'way of thinking' that benefits you.

Once you have integrated this way of thinking for yourself, the next step is to look at how emotional intelligence could affect your relationships with others. By increasing your ability to listen more deeply and be more engaged, you will become more empathetic and influential. By remembering not just a person's name but key facts in conversations, the emotions they are demonstrating and the subtext of their intentions, you model a greater appreciation of people. This often has the fortuitous side effect of creating greater rapport.

'All learning has an emotional base.'

Plato

MAPPING YOUR EMOTIONAL INTELLIGENCE

Think of a person whom you regard as in touch with him- or herself and socially adept, the type of person who easily builds rapport. This person may also be a leader. On a scale of 1 to 10, if they are a 10, where are you in terms of:

▶ your current ability?

▶ your potential?

▶ your goal for three months' time?

Mark the point where you rate your emotional intelligence (towards yourself and socially) on the scale below.

1_____10

What would it mean to you to be smarter emotionally?

→ What would happen if you could increase your performance by 10–50 per cent?

_____

→ How would this make you feel?

_____

→ What current challenges do you face?

_____

Using your notes, give yourself five minutes to create your thoughts, making visual notes in the following space.

→ Overcoming problems

As an actor back in the early 1990s, I was introduced to the world of memory techniques after completing a two-week audio course. As mentioned at the beginning of this book, shortly after this I received a call from my agent looking for game show ideas for a friend who worked at a London production company, Action Time. Being an actor and my 23-year-old self, I never said no to anything, so I responded by saying, 'Give me 30 minutes.' Half an hour later I had written up a format for a memory game show where ordinary people from all walks of life could perform extraordinary feats of memory.

In my first meeting with the head of Action Time, the question came up of who would train the contestants. Again, my actorly instincts and my 23-year-old self felt compelled to say, 'I will.' In essence, I jumped in at the deep end, giving myself what felt like a massive challenge. I decided to commit totally, go with it, work to hone my skills and go from 'confident' to 'competent'. This was a steep learning curve.

What steep learning curve have you experienced in your life? When you think about the challenges or problems that have come up, how do you see them? Were they barriers that got in your way, held you back and blocked you? Or were they the opportunities that challenged you to break through and increase your sphere of knowledge?

Whether we refer to the situations that present themselves as problems, challenges, or something else, these interesting events that happen throughout our lives compel us to learn and grow. If we avoid our problems, more often than not, instead of going away, they just tend to get bigger and bigger, causing stress and anxiety. We can sometimes avoid them for a long time, but sooner or later they will force us to act.

Perhaps you have had the experience where you put off an appointment and kept on doing so until you knew you just 'had' to do it. Once a person has overcome a particular challenge, it no longer seems like such a big problem when they are faced with something similar; in fact, we can relish and look forward to it. At this point we are confident *and* competent.

Have you ever been in the situation where you have started a new job in which you have minimal experience but a sense that it could be a good fit? Did it ever feel daunting or even overwhelming? Was there ever a time when you felt that you were 'winging it' and afraid that you would be found out?

 Exercise 88

 GROWING PAINS

Think of some events that have happened in your life, which at the time seemed like large problems but, looking back on them now, you realize actually helped you increase your skills and knowledge. They were challenges that shaped who you have become.

Add them to the sketch below, inside the circle.

What great problems do you have in your life right now that could create opportunities for learning new skills and grow your knowledge?

Add these challenges to the above sketch outside the circle.

→ Memory and decision making

How do you decide how to tackle a problem? What part does your memory play in this process? We have all heard the saying, 'One day I'll look back and laugh at this.' Somewhere in this idea is the notion that, given time, you will remember the experience from a different perspective from the one you have as you are going through it.

In his 2010 TED Talk 'The riddle of experience vs memory', Daniel Kahneman talks about the remembering self (the story of our life) and the experiencing self (in the present). There are differences between what we experience and what we remember the experience to be, the latter having an effect on the decisions we make.

> *'We don't choose between experiences, we choose between memories of experiences. Even when we think about the future, we don't think of our future normally as experiences. We think of our future as anticipated memories.'*
>
> Daniel Kahneman

If we accept Kahneman's idea, then the memory of your experiences can influence how you evaluate a problem and make decisions about it. If you have a past memory that supports you in overcoming that problem, it can help guide you to make good decisions. If you can't find a useful reference, then creating a future memory could help you do the same thing.

This is in line with the Pareto Principle you memorized back in Exercise 46: your focus should be 20 per cent on the problem and 80 per cent on the solution. The previous activity may already represent that 20 per cent. Potentially there could be more to flesh out so that the problem is completely understood. In order to focus on the solution you can start by creating this anticipated future memory.

If you want to become smarter at public speaking, you might first create a future memory where you give a great speech incorporating strategies you already use for creative memorization to help make the scene come alive. Once that memory is there, you can then 'chunk back' to figure out the strategy that got you there and the decisions that you made. This focuses the majority of your time (the 80 per cent) on the solution and also puts you in a more resourceful state.

CREATING FUTURE MEMORIES

This activity uses a simple scaling model to create your future memory and build a set of decisions and strategies towards it. Look at how you may adapt or create your own take on this idea.

Choose one of the problems you identified in the previous activity, and write it below.

_____

What future anticipated memory could you design that would see you having overcome this problem? Describe it in detail as if it has already happened; get your emotions involved and see, hear and feel what is taking place.

_____

_____

_____

Below is the problem scale, where number 10 represents your future memory, in which you have completely overcome the problem and increased your knowledge or skills.

1_____10

If number 10 is where you want to get to, where are you now? Make a mark on the scale and describe this in detail here:

_____

_____

_____

Chunk up one number at a time when designing your plan so, if you are at a 5, draw the number 6. Ask yourself what you need to do to get to number 6.

What are the things that could get you to 10 more effectively?

Check that your decisions are being influenced by your future memory, capturing any notes in the space below.

→ Red alert!

Having a way to control your stress and anxiety levels can be a positive strategy to support your memory and your health. To do this, we need to be aware of a structure in both hemispheres of the brain called the amygdala, which is the size of a small almond. As previously mentioned, it is the emotional specialist of the brain. Whereas the hippocampus will catalogue episodic memory, the amygdala catalogues your emotional memories.

The amygdala is also responsible for the well-known 'fight or flight' response, your brain's red-alert system. Once activated, this emotional response overrides other parts of the brain, including the prefrontal cortex, responsible for logic and reasoning. The psychologist Daniel Goleman coined the term 'amygdala hijack' to describe an overwhelming emotional response to a stimulus, citing as an example the story of Mike Tyson biting Evander Holyfield's ear after becoming enraged during a boxing match in 1997.

What experiences of an amygdala hijacking have you had in your life? What was your instinct – to fight or flee, to fly or jump in? This hijacking can also happen if you are under a lot of pressure: if you have to get a report in fast or if relationships at work are not going well. When you think of these things, your amygdala will want to get involved and you start to focus on whether to 'deal with' the problem or try to avoid it. If these feelings last for prolonged periods of time, anxiety and stress can result. To avoid this, it is useful to have a way to control your amygdala and release those anxieties.

Exercise 90

RELEASING ANXIETY

Rather than target a specific stressful situation, this quick technique entails using your visual, auditory and sensory skills to shift anxious feelings and release the fears connected with them.

Take a moment to think about any fears or anxieties you have, about either learning new knowledge and skills or your memory in general.

Capture your top three for learning and memory below.

→ **Learning**

1 _____

2 _____

3 _____

→ Memory

1 _____

2 _____

3 _____

By running through the following simple visualization, you will create new connections to some of the feelings you have associated with learning and memory. Initially these may have come from a memory of a childhood experience at school or some other event, or from many events throughout your life.

Imagine the following:

▶ Think about the fears, stresses or anxieties you captured in your lists above. Take a moment and imagine where those feelings are in your body… connect with these feelings and start to notice where they live. Perhaps they are in your stomach, chest or neck, or maybe it's a general feeling all over your body.

▶ Now you know where they are, go to the place where the feelings are most intense. This might be at its centre, on the side, on top or somewhere else. As you focus on this part, describe out loud to yourself what it feels like. As it becomes clearer, take some deep breaths… If it was a good friend, how differently might you feel… take a moment and spend some time with it…

▶ You may start to notice that the feelings you had in this area of your body are becoming somewhat different; perhaps you feel more neutral about them, more relaxed or even happy. Breathe deeply and stay with this new feeling you have now for a moment or two…

▶ Think about the list you wrote down and decide whether any of your answers still seem accurate, or would you now create a different list for learning and memory? You may now choose to stay with this feeling for some time, until you are ready to become aware of your surroundings again.

Go to www.achieve-with.me/memoryworkbook where you can go through the visualization in more detail.

→ Only connect

Being emotionally intelligent does not only relate to understanding yourself. It is also about your interactions with others: how you connect, empathize, lead and influence. There are more and more opportunities than ever before to reach out and connect with people. With this opportunity comes the challenge of remembering details that can help you make deeper connections and potentially make a positive impact in your life. That could be a recommendation for a job, working with someone on a new idea or overcoming relationship challenges.

REMEMBERING NAMES

It is common to take it for granted that we won't always remember the name of someone we have just met. A belief that we are 'just no good with names' can hold us back so much that, rather than try and fail, we avoid even attempting to remember names in the first place.

Other reasons for this can come into play: the complexity of a name, difficulty of pronunciation and, of course, the one which probably happens more than any other – you are introduced to someone and then realize you were not really 'listening' for their name. Rather than ask again, you hope it will somehow come up in conversation. These are all fairly standard responses and culturally it is almost the norm.

When someone is good at remembering names, then, it can have a very positive impact. People like being remembered – it makes them feel good and gives them a sense that you are truly interested in them. This offers possibilities to build deeper rapport. Have you ever noticed that when a person is good with names, you tend to remember them? This is because they are usually also good at giving you attention, really listening and focusing on what you are saying. This type of person tends to approach the challenge of names from a different perspective.

NAMES AND YOU

To find out your strengths and weaknesses when it comes to remembering names, read the statements below.

Tick the boxes next to the statements that best describe you.

Challenges
- ☐ I just can't remember names!
- ☐ I don't think I pay attention.
- ☐ I miss hearing the name.
- ☐ If there are too many people, I don't bother.
- ☐ I remember it initially but it's gone within ten minutes.
- ☐ I'm great at remembering faces but not names.
- ☐ If the name is complex, I won't even try to remember it.

What I do now
- ☐ I am a natural at remembering names.
- ☐ I am interested in knowing who people are.
- ☐ I listen intently.
- ☐ I love it when I remember lots of people in one go.
- ☐ I can meet someone months later and still remember their name.
- ☐ I remember the person (their face, their name and usually some details).
- ☐ I love the challenge of remembering a name I've never heard before.

Did you tick more in the 'Challenges' column or the 'What I do now' column? Your results should give you a simple view of where your strengths and weaknesses lie when it comes to remembering names.

→ The right mindset

How curious are you when you meet someone new? In order for you to remember a person, it probably goes without saying that it is a great help to be genuinely interested in them. With this interest, you prime your brain to look for natural connections and put yourself in their shoes. This allows you to inhabit a person's world and start to experience it from their point of view. When you experience meeting someone at this level, you immediately listen more intently and make strong internal connections as you reflect and abstract your thoughts.

You can cultivate this mindset even with people who don't immediately interest you. Being able to achieve this state can be as simple as asking yourself this question: What is interesting about this person?

By asking this or something similar, with a positive expectation, your internal search engine starts to look for the answers. (Remember your Google brain.) You will be looking at them in a different way, taking in more of their features and expressions; they might even remind you of someone or something.

Through creative memorization, you can utilize this experience. Actively contemplate how you might make a connection between what this person looks like and what their name is going to be, as a way of pre-empting the problem of 'I remember the face but I can't remember the name.' For some people, this will mean exaggerating a feature (let us say they have a distinctive nose), telling yourself who they remind you of (he looks exactly like a mad scientist!) or comparing them to an object (they remind me of a teapot!). It almost goes without saying that you should avoid telling people the connections you are making in your mind!

LISTENING

The previous two steps should all happen in an instant, after which you will meet the person and hear their name. All you have to do here is listen. Interestingly, this is probably the point that many people miss, perhaps because they are busy thinking about something else and not properly primed. If you are in the right mindset, you should be ready to take this on board.

MAKING A CONNECTION

You have the right mindset, you have listened and now you need to connect. There isn't just one way to do this, so find a strategy that works for you and is in line with your learning style and preferences. The most important thing is that you make a connection by associating their appearance with their name in some way.

For example, you meet someone called Kiefer who reminded you of a mad scientist before you heard his name. In this case, you could make the following associations.

▶ Imagine it was Kiefer Sutherland in a new role.

▶ Attach the image of a Key covered in fur to his distinctive nose.

▶ Tell yourself that it's Crazy Kiefer.

As you make your connection, like any reference story you will want to hear what it sounds like and know what it feels like to say 'Nice to meet you, Kiefer.' While saying the name, you will be thinking and visualizing your connection. In order to strengthen this connection, look to use the name in conversation in a way that is natural and appropriate.

If someone's name is completely new to you, ask if they mind telling you it again. By asking, you are immediately showing an interest in something that is personal and important to them. If all else fails, ask them to spell it, letting them know that you like to get people's names right, and then check that you have it right.

CONDITIONING

The challenge with this process will be to put it into practice consistently. When you meet new people, you could well be focusing on something completely different, so you will need a small 'nudge' to remind you to spend a few seconds putting this strategy into practice. Refer back to Exercise 77 on memory triggers and create a memory trigger that will immediately get you into the right mindset so that you are ready to listen and connect. If you can condition yourself to do this, it will soon be wired up into your natural way of thinking.

 Exercise 92

MEETING THE TEAM

It's your first day in a new job. You are being shown around and introduced to the team. Everything feels as if it is on fast-forward. What would it be like if you could actually remember all the people you are meeting, the people you are about to spend a good chunk of your life with?

The following names and faces were used in the World Memory Championship competition. Imagine that these are a group of new work colleagues you are meeting for the first time.

Names and Faces Memorisation Paper

Ichiro Hussein   Genzeb Wolf   Alejandro Putin   Rachele Jabr   David Chai

Suzy Tsakhiagiin   Batsaikhan Yeats   Haifa Villaraigosa   Olga Besud

Give yourself 15 minutes and see how many names you can remember. Without looking at the images, write down their names here.

1 _____

2 _____

3 _____

4 _____

5 _____

6 _____

7 _____

8 _____

9 _____

When checking your results, identify the areas where you need to improve. What other strategies could you use that would be more personal to you and your learning style? Capture your thoughts below.

_____

_____

_____

_____

_____

→ # Active listening

Have you ever been in a conversation or meeting when you know you 'understand' what's being said, but it's just not going in? When you try to relay the details to someone else, you are unable to do so in a succinct manner.

Active listening is a term used in many different fields to describe a deeper level of listening and interaction. At its core are the following ideas:

1 You are completely 'in the moment' and engaging with the other person, focusing all your attention on what they are saying.

2 You are listening on many different levels, including the facts of the conversation, the feelings that you are seeing and hearing, and the intentions and subtext you are deriving.

3 You are actively responding to the other person in terms of your body language and your vocal acknowledgements, which include things like, 'Uh huh', 'Yes, I see' and 'Mmm', all of which should come from a real place and not be forced.

Active listening also incorporates strategies around **reflecting back** what you might hear, see or perceive. Before reflecting, you have to have established a good level of rapport. In a coaching model you may use this technique to raise awareness of a belief or behaviour a person has. For example, if you said something like, 'Have you noticed that whenever you talk about your upcoming exam you put your head in your hands?', you offer the coachee a chance to evaluate what that means to them.

Paraphrasing is another technique in active listening. This is where you will play something back to a person in your own words, usually to clarify their meaning or intention. For example, if your coachee says, 'I'm snowed under at work, there is just so much information to deal with, and don't even get me started on email. And my boss is on my back so, with all of this going on, there's no time to think!' You may paraphrase this by saying, 'So I'm hearing you have more work than you feel you can handle and you want to create time to think? Is that right?' This may or may not be what the coachee meant, but by phrasing this in your own words it helps to clarify meaning for both of you.

Another active listening strategy is simply to **summarize** the conversation. 'We've talked about work overload, what you want and the next action you are going to take, is that right?' Summarizing helps to pinpoint what has actually been talked about and what will happen next.

You might use some or all of these strategies, depending on the situation and what works for you. If you did nothing else except employ active listening, you would notice a dramatic increase in your ability to remember more of the conversations you have, and with whom. You would also notice that there would be less need for reams of notes and a greater chance of building rapport.

Exercise 93

CREATIVE LISTENING

Creative listening is when you incorporate active listening and creative memorization to heighten the memories of your conversations with people. You can choose to dial this up and down to whatever level is suitable for the situation.

Study the following image for two or three minutes. From the previous description of active listening, reflect on what you think it means in the context of a conversation with another person and what its purpose could be.

Capture your ideas below.

_____

_____

_____

_____

_____

→ Combining techniques

As we have seen, when we listen to a conversation, we are often thinking about how we might respond, or perhaps we are just listening on the surface or distracted by something else. Being able to listen on a deeper level can increase focus, get you into the state of flow and help you to naturally remember more.

Exercise 93 shows how creative listening uses active listening techniques and combines them with creative memorization. Let us look at each individual part of the process and how everything fits together.

STEP 1: LISTEN ON MANY LEVELS

Many people, during a conversation, will be listening only to what is on the surface. In active listening you want to listen at many different levels: to what is on the surface – the **facts** – and to what is under the surface – the emotions and **feelings** being expressed. During the conversation is there some subtext, a deeper **intention** beneath the facts? By increasing the scope of what a person listens to, you increase the chances of understanding and remembering more of what is being said. This is what listening to **facts**, **feelings** and **intentions** means.

STEP 2: REFLECT, PARAPHRASE, SUMMARIZE

Reflecting, paraphrasing and summarizing are your tools for gaining clarity, honing your thoughts and dialling up your memory. By also using the person's language and learning style when reflecting, paraphrasing and summarizing, you make sure you continue to build a connection and maintain clarity. Phrases like 'The way I see it, …' suggest a visual style, 'By the sound of it,' an auditory preference, and 'It feels like we should…' a kinaesthetic preference. When responding, you can build rapport by matching their style, saying, 'It looks like you want to explore…', 'I'm hearing you say…' or 'I feel that your approach is to…'

STEP 3: BE A DETECTIVE

If you reflect on your experience throughout this workbook, you will have noticed that questions are key. In the context of social interactions, an effective metaphor is to become a detective, perhaps like that classic TV character Columbo. As you question, people automatically search and reflect, allowing you to build up a memorable picture employing the techniques in step 2. While questioning in itself is a big topic, two useful types of question to keep in mind are open and closed questions. In the context of creative memorization, you could think of them in the following way:

- **Open questions** search for facts, options, solutions, areas of mutual benefit and understanding.
- **Closed questions** get confirmation and clarity.

Examples of open questions are:

- What makes you want to improve your memory?
- As you are reading this, what answer comes to mind?

These questions make you search for an answer that is more than just a simple yes or no. If someone were to respond saying, 'I don't know', you could continue to ask open questions, like, 'If you did know, what would it be?' or 'What do you think makes those memory guys want to improve their memory?' or 'What are the differences between how you think and how they think?' You become the detective!

Examples of closed questions are:

- Do you feel good about that?
- Are you committed?
- Is this working?
- Do you follow me?

These will elicit only an explicit yes or no response.

 Get creative

In active listening, where does creative memorization fit in?

While you are listening, your complete focus should be on the individual speaking. As they speak, you will naturally have images and connections that come to mind, but let them happen and keep your focus on the individual.

Your opportunity to 'dial it up' is when you are reflecting, paraphrasing, summarizing and questioning. At this point you are completely active and you can let your imagination paint pictures, hear symphonies and touch emotions. By doing this, you are employing all the SAVI principles, accelerating your understanding and making the experience truly memorable. You can even have a set of memory networks to store some of the key facts that you play back.

My preference is to use iMind and project what is happening internally out in front of me. This keeps me in the moment. You will discover what is right for you.

Exercise 94

HAVING A CREATIVE CONVERSATION

Practise this exercise with a friend, partner or colleague.

Ask your friend to pick a subject that they know really well and to explain it to you. Use creative memorization to understand and remember as much of it as possible. You may find that the person you are talking with reveals some hidden 'gems'.

After the conversation, create a visual note below that captures what you remember.

→ Out and about

If you work in a café or restaurant or elsewhere in a service industry, being able to remember customers' orders is an important skill, especially for your regulars. In the early pilot show of my game show *Memory Masters*, contestants had to memorize an entire pizza menu, take an order from a table of ten people and then remember each person's starter, main course, dessert and drink all at once, and then serve the right meal to the right person. We showed them some memory techniques and their results were fairly impressive.

It can be fun to try this out when you are out in a social situation with a group of friends. The following activity will test your ability to remember ten people, the meal they ordered and the drink they had.

Exercise 95

WHOSE ROUND?

You can practise the skill of remembering an order any time you are out, at a restaurant or perhaps buying a round of drinks.

Imagine that ten people sitting round a table have ordered the following food and drinks.

Customer	Order
Diane	Pepperoni pizza & diet Coke
Marcia	Spaghetti bolognese & red wine
Robert	Mussels & white wine
Ian	Roast chicken & lemonade
Susan	Beef Wellington & beer
Joshua	Veggie burger & apple juice
Harry	Tomato soup & water
Lucy	Apple pie & tea
Stuart	Ham & cheese sandwich & coffee
James	Hot dog & strawberry milkshake

Without writing down any reference stories, choose a method to memorize their names, meals and drinks.

Cover the orders above and match up the correct meal and drink with the right person. Write your answers against the names in the diagram below.

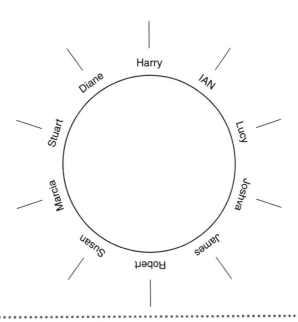

→ Your social networks

The previous exercises are all focused on your interactions with others in face-to-face situations. With an improved memory for names, faces and personal facts, you can make the most of your social networks. Using social media like Facebook and LinkedIn can help you become more prepared for interviews or meetings with potential clients, or you can simply use your social networks as a fun way to practise and hone your skills.

Summary

In this chapter you explored the world of emotions in relation to understanding yourself and your interactions with others. You have practised strategies to remember names and become 'laser focused' when it comes to conversations. Go back to Exercise 87 and mark the point on the scale where you feel you are now, and make changes to your potential as well if necessary.

Emotion can be a powerful tonic when it comes to creating memories that last. Think about where the skills and strategies in this chapter could make an impact in your life, personally and professionally.

What I have learned

What are my thoughts, feelings and insights on what I have read so far?

_____

_____

_____

Use the space below to summarize the actions to take as a result of reading this chapter.

_____

_____

_____

_____

Where to next?

Over the last six chapters you have seen how memory can help you perform smarter with words, numbers, music, pictures, body and emotions. The next chapter will take you through a training programme based on the games at the World Memory Championships and will culminate in you designing your own programme to keep yourself memory fit.

12
Your memory workout

In this chapter you will learn:
▶ how to do a mental warm-up to get you 'in the memory zone'
▶ a speed memory workout
▶ a stamina memory workout.

Now that you have experienced ways to perform smarter in six key areas of intelligence, you need to stay in shape, continuing to master your memory so that you can perform smarter when it counts. This chapter is designed to give you ideas on how to create your own memory gym, consisting of short high-impact mini-memory workouts and longer stamina sessions to keep your skills honed.

You could think of these memory workouts as training for a race – let's say a marathon. The act of going out and running every day will certainly help keep you fit and healthy, make a difference to your energy levels, help you learn about yourself, know how far you can push yourself and open your eyes to your potential. When you train for a marathon, your outcomes are focused, with this focus comes motivation and with motivation come results. In this sense the memory workouts should do the same thing: take you towards your goals.

'*Learning never exhausts the mind.*'

Leonardo da Vinci

Here is Jill's mind map from exercise 6 as an Example of how to create your own vision.

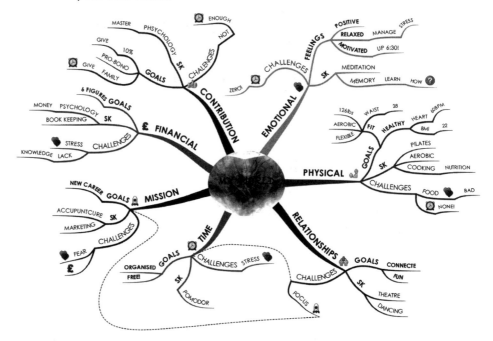

Your version should paint a clear picture of the goals, challenges, skills and knowledge you need to grow in order to achieve your results. Think about the strategies you have learned and spend some time updating your map. Keep it somewhere you can see it, to give you focus and to remind you why you are spending time keeping memory fit.

The World Memory Championships

The World Memory Championships came into being in 1991, through Tony Buzan and Raymond Keene. 'Why,' asked Tony, 'when there are competitions for almost everything else, are there no competitions for memory, the most important function of the brain?'

The two men invited the top memorizers in the world at that time to compete for the title of World Memory Champion. This competition, called *Memoriad '91*, took place in London in front of over 100 spectators, journalists and film crews. The event made a star of the first winner, Dominic O'Brien, who went on to win a total of eight times.

The sport is now practised in over 30 countries. To become an official Grand Master of Memory, you have to compete in one of the memory competitions that takes place around the world. At the time of writing you would have to be able to remember sequences of 1,000 numbers in an hour, 520 cards (10 packs) in an hour and a single pack of cards in two minutes.

→ The workout of champions

The following workouts are based on games from the World Memory Championships, with some variations for training purposes. The games are split into warm-ups, speed training and stamina training, and each one includes master tips on how to increase your performance.

Once you have experienced these games, you can design your personal daily workout, set your targets and log your progress, focusing on building up your memory in the areas of intelligence you most want to improve and perform well in.

PREPARATION

Before you begin, you will need to have created a set of memory networks. Around 100 are enough to get you started. If you are training daily, then 300 will let you swap your networks each day so that images have time to fade.

For each workout you do, first run the workout and then record your results.

TIME ALLOCATION

Have you ever made a New Year's resolution to get down to the gym and then you do, only to overdo it, waking up the next morning aching all over and trying to claim back your gym membership? You might have a similar approach to memory workouts, but it's important to think small chunks to begin with and build up over time.

Aim for 15 minutes a day three to five times a week for the first three weeks. This is enough to get you into the swing of it and leave you wanting more. After three weeks you should aim to do up to 30 minutes for your warm-up and speed sessions, with your choice of stamina session up to three times a week.

→ Your workout menu

Before starting, take a moment to get an overview of each workout.
Check off the ones below that seem interesting to you or which grab
your attention.

Warm-ups

☐ Energize

☐ N-Back

☐ Story cubes

☐ Recognition drills

☐ Relativistic training

☐ Metaphors

Speed games

☐ Five-minute words

☐ Five-minute numbers

☐ Five-minute cards

☐ Five-minute names

☐ Top five stories

☐ Quote of the day

☐ Top three tracks

Stamina games

☐ 30-minute numbers

☐ 30-minute cards

☐ 20 foreign words

☐ The speech

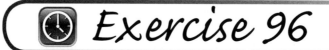

Exercise 96

WARM-UPS

As with any form of exercise, it's good practice to warm up first. For
memory training you want to get yourself into a positive, relaxed and
energized state. Before you begin, find a place where you will be
able to focus for five to ten minutes, turn your phone off and remove
anything that could be distracting. You want to get used to this being
a time when you can be completely present in the moment.

Ideally, first warm-ups should become habitual, so make sure you
don't overdo it in the beginning. It is fine to do only a couple of rounds
at first, and then build slowly over time as your stamina increases.

Here are your choices of warm-ups. You can decide on just one,
several or all of them. If you do only warm-ups, this would be enough
to keep your skills to a level where you could continue to incorporate
this new way of thinking into your daily life.

Energize

This exercise, from Tony Robbin's Personal Power programme, uses a deep diaphragmatic breath to stimulate the lymphatic system, essential for removing waste from cells. By practising this breathing before working out you will energize your body and feel sharp.

▶ Breathe at this ratio: in for one, hold for four, out for two. (If you breathe in for four counts you would hold for 16 and breathe out for eight.)
▶ Repeat the process ten times.

N-Back

Since creative memorization depends on your working memory, this is a good place to start in order to get yourself into that state of flow. Revisit Exercise 15 to experience the N-Back task.

Story cubes

Story cubes should be familiar to you from Chapter 4. This warm-up should take under 30 seconds for one pack of cubes. You can stretch yourself by adding different types of packs.

▶ Roll the dice.
▶ Either place the dice randomly into a sequence and then memorize the sequence, or choose one dice at a time, crafting the story as you go.
▶ Test your recall.

Recognition drills

Recognition drills are all about becoming quicker at recognizing the various visual languages you have developed for memory networks, numbers, cards or anything else. You are conditioning your brain to recognize a language without thinking about it, so the process of 'decoding' is eventually bypassed. In the case of a number, when you see 22 you just know it means 'Nun' without having to go via the phonetic system to work it out. Let us look at a choice of three recognition drills in a bit more detail.

1 **Network drills: If you want to be able to memorize at speed, whether in training, competition or perhaps even in a meeting, having a memory network you can zip through is probably the easiest way. This short exercise aims to increase your speed**

at going to each file in your network. In Exercise 24, Remote control, you viewed the chains you created in fast-forward and then rewind, and for speed networks you use the same principle: run through the network on fast-forward, then rewind, each time increasing the speed.

  ▷ Choose one or several memory networks.

  ▷ Use the remote control until you are ready to time.

  ▷ Start a stopwatch and capture your time. Use this as a benchmark for you to beat in your next session.

2 **Number drills:** Practising number drills is fairly straightforward. You can choose how many numbers to start with; beginning with 100 is probably a good opening place. For each two-digit number, see the relevant image in your mind. In the sequence of numbers below this could translate to: cake, mummy, shot, nam, can, fame, num, nero, nam, sin for the first line. Remember, you are not memorizing but purely seeing the images in your mind.

  ▷ Set a timer to two minutes.

  ▷ See as many images as you can until the timer runs out.

  ▷ Count up how far you got (this is your score to beat).

  ▷ Once you can do 100, move up to 200 and so on.

7	7	3	3	6	1	2	3	7	2	8	3	2	2	2	4	2	3	0	2
7	7	1	1	2	5	7	2	8	2	4	9	9	0	9	5	1	1	9	2
0	9	2	1	8	3	2	9	0	7	5	2	7	8	2	9	5	8	9	8
4	8	0	1	2	3	8	3	1	5	1	9	8	3	1	8	5	4	9	9
6	2	7	8	7	4	4	5	6	7	4	2	5	1	7	9	1	9	7	2
9	9	0	7	3	4	9	0	5	9	2	9	5	7	8	3	1	5	6	9
7	0	1	9	8	0	0	7	8	8	1	9	7	5	3	6	8	2	4	1
1	3	2	0	4	1	8	0	5	4	6	6	8	0	8	0	4	7	6	5
7	3	1	6	3	2	8	6	4	3	3	1	6	7	7	3	2	0	6	9
8	4	2	5	3	1	0	3	7	8	7	9	6	3	3	5	9	5	4	7

3 Card drills: To run card drills, you first have to create an image for every card in the pack similar to the number system. Since you already know the phonetic system, this is a good way to start learning how to memorize a pack of cards. Cards, like cubes, are tactile objects that are great for giving you a quick workout.

The following card system uses phonetics. For each card, you start with the first letter of each suit. D is for Diamonds, H is for Hearts, C is for Clubs and S is for Spades. You then use the numbers 1 to 9 for Ace to 9 and the number zero for the number 10. From these you can start to create images for cards.

▷ **Three of diamonds is DaM – D for diamonds and M is three.**

▷ **Ten of hearts is HoSe – H for hearts and S for ten.**

For the picture cards you can choose whether you want to use a code, such as DJ for Jack of Diamonds – one of your favourite DJs – or you use a more natural association as with the Queens and Kings below, made personal to you.

▷ **Queen of diamonds: the Queen**

▷ **Queen of hearts: the good witch from *The Wizard of Oz***

▷ **Queen of clubs: the bad witch from *The Wizard of Oz***

▷ **Queen of spades: Bellatrix Lestrange from *Harry Potter***

Number	Diamonds	Hearts	Clubs	Spades
Ace	Data	Hat	Cat	Sat
2	Dan	Han	Can	Sin
3	Dam	Ham	Cameo	Sam
4	Dare	Hair	Car	Soar
5	Doll	Hail	Call	Sail
6	Dash	Hash	Cash	Sash
7	Duck	Hack	Cake	Sack
8	Dave	Hoof	Café	Sofa
9	Debbie	Hop	Cap	Sap
10	Daz	Hose	Case	Sas
J	DJ	Hey Jude	Cajole	SJ
Q	The Queen	Good witch	Bad witch	Bellatrix
K	The King	The wizard	Captain Caveman	Voldemort

To run a recognition drill for your cards, follow these steps:

▶ First start with an even, slow rhythm, moving your finger from one card to the next in any pattern you wish (depicted below: slow motion to begin with).

▶ As you move from card to card, say the image of the card out loud.

▶ If you can't remember a card, simply move on to the next.

▶ Gradually increase your speed, continuing to speak each image aloud.

▶ Continue for three minutes.

▶ At the end, identify any of the cards that caused you problems and 'dial them up'.

Relativistic training

When Tony Buzan was talking about relativistic training, he told this simple story. Imagine you are driving a car on the motorway at 70 mph and I ask you to take the next exit. As you do, I cover the speedometer and ask you to slow down to 30 mph. What speed do you think you will actually slow down to? Most likely it will be faster than 30 mph, perhaps 40–50; this will 'feel' like 30 because you have been going so fast.

This idea is used a lot for learning speed-reading, and it is also perfect for improving your memorizing speed during workouts.

▶ Choose a recognition drill workout such as a network drill.

▶ Start off slowly and increase your speed.

- Keep increasing your speed until you lose all comprehension.
- Slow it down so you gain comprehension and then speed it up until you lose it again.
- Repeat this process at a high intensity for up to three minutes.

Once you get used to this technique, you can try it out on your speed workouts. It will help to increase the speed at which you can 'associate' images together.

Metaphors

This is where you can play with your creative abilities. You will need to use a pack of story cubes.

- Set a timer for three minutes.
- Roll the dice, pick out any three and line them up.
- Let us say the three images on the dice are a chalice, a tent and a map.
- How could you connect these three images together to represent something else?

Example: 'There is a King who never leaves his tent, spending day after day protecting his magic chalice of wealth for fear someone might steal it, even though a wise old man had left him a map that could lead him to a richer, happier life.'

What does this visual metaphor mean to you? How might you relate it to your own or someone else's life?

_____

_____

· ·

PLANNING YOUR WARM-UPS

Plan your warm-ups for the next seven days. The number you do per day is entirely up to you but, however many you choose, make a commitment to yourself to follow through. If you are in doubt, then do the minimum number possible and slowly build up the habit. Once you have completed the exercises, tick them off to track your progress. In addition, leave some time to commit to at least one speed workout and one stamina workout over the next seven days.

Day	Activities	Completed
1		
2		
3		
4		
5		
6		
7		

Exercise 97

SPEED GAMES

The following are short examples of speed games, based on events in the World Memory Championships. Add some or all of them to your daily workouts.

Five-minute words

Memorize as many words as you can in five minutes.

▶ Start your timer.

▶ Memorize the words in sequence, using any method you wish.

▶ Score a point for each one until you make a mistake (if you get the first five correct and the sixth one wrong, you only score five points, even if the rest are correct).

Random words				
· earth	· lord	· evening	· tonic	· plastic bag
· dinosaur	· string	· corn	· loop	· crown
· policeman	· giant	· observation	· orange	· herb
· bikini	· diary	· stamp	· crown	· verse
· fur	· sheet	· printer	· shark	· sticky tape
· stamp	· elephant	· Olympics	· library	· queen
· merit	· croissant	· film	· ambiguous	· synthetic
· brass	· picture	· tap	· tiger	· nest
Total score:				

Generated by http://creativitygames.net/random-word-generator

Five-minute numbers

Memorize as many numbers as you can in five minutes. Start with 100 digits.

▶ Start the timer.

▶ Working across the rows, associate each number to a file on one of your memory networks.

▶ Check for speed and accuracy.

▶ Score 20 points for every correct line. If you make one mistake in a line, you lose ten points; if you make two mistakes, you lose the whole line.

0	8	8	1	3	2	4	2	6	4	1	6	7	0	3	4	2	7	0	0
5	2	5	7	4	5	4	7	8	1	1	2	0	0	7	6	6	1	7	6
5	5	8	3	4	3	7	0	4	3	6	0	2	7	1	1	8	5	6	4
1	9	5	9	9	8	3	4	0	1	4	8	8	7	3	9	6	7	3	8
3	3	5	3	0	7	7	2	8	2	6	1	4	9	3	6	1	0	2	4

Five-minute cards

This is similar to the five-minute number workout, but with cards.

▶ Start the timer.

▶ Memorize in sequence as many cards as you can in five minutes.

▶ If you finish in less than five minutes, record your time and how many you recalled correctly.

▶ If you run out of time, count up how many you recalled correctly up to that point.

Five-minute names

With the aid of the Internet, it is fairly easy to give yourself a small workout with names. You should also have plenty of opportunity to practise this in your day-to-day life.

- ▶ Use a site with a members' directory, such as Equity: www.equity.org.uk/directory-of-members/
- ▶ Find the list of names.
- ▶ Start the timer.
- ▶ Memorize as many names as you can in five minutes.
- ▶ Give yourself a point for every first or last name you get correctly.

Top five stories

If you are used to reading a newspaper in the morning, this will take a minimal amount of time. Use a method that feels right to you to memorize your top five news story headlines. The purpose here isn't to use creative memorization to remember the whole story, but just a simple image of the headline to spark off what the story was about.

Try it out with these news stories:

- ▶ Kepler telescope spies 'most Earth-like' worlds to date
  http://www.bbc.co.uk/news/science-environment-22200476
- ▶ Wearable technology: The bra designed to shock attackers
  http://www.bbc.co.uk/news/business-22110443
- ▶ Super-powered battery breakthrough claimed by US team
  http://www.bbc.co.uk/news/technology-22191650
- ▶ Footage reveals how insects use their bodies to hover
  http://www.bbc.co.uk/news/science-environment-22130854
- ▶ Dinosaur 'fills fossil record gap'
  http://www.bbc.co.uk/news/science-environment-22210435

A good tip is to use the image beside the story as a file and connect that to a keyword in the title. For the Kepler telescope story, you might imagine a spy with a telescope standing on the planet in the picture beside the story. In essence, the picture in the story becomes your mental file.

Quote of the day

Use the strategy from Exercise 49, Using quotes, to remember just one quote. A good resource for this is www.goodreads.com/quotes

Top three tracks

Use your favourite chart site to tag your top three music tracks, using the strategy from Exercise 69, Remembering the top tracks.

PLANNING YOUR SPEED WORKOUTS

Think about each of the speed workouts described and choose the ones you believe you can commit to over the next seven days, along with your memory warm-ups. Then add these to the planning table above.

→ Moving into the big league

Stamina training takes you into the big league as a memorizer. Like any stamina event, it can be very challenging but extremely satisfying when you complete it. Like relativistic training, once you have completed some stamina events, the speed exercises and warm-ups will feel easy in comparison. This can have a major impact when you apply creative memorization to something which gives you value, as your brain will be wired to working at a much higher level than you need for performing at most tasks, such as remembering key information in a conversation, visual cues for a presentation or statistics to bring to a meeting. All of a sudden this feels like child's play.

When I first competed in the World Memory Championships, I memorized 400 consecutive images in one hour (800 digits). I made four mistakes so lost 56 digits, which meant I scored a total of 744 numbers. Although it might not seem that memorizing a 400-digit number is all that useful, it builds your 'capability' to perform at a high level.

Grand Master of Memory Ed Cooke, who helped Joshua Foer, author of *Moonwalking with Einstein,* has a fantastic online community where you can easily build your memory skills and share your own creations with others. Memrise is a community where you can grow your knowledge in pretty much any area, including languages. www.memrise.com

STAMINA GAMES

While having a single image for remembering numbers from 00 to 99 is probably sufficient for most purposes, if numbers are key to your role and certainly if you are aiming for a competition, you may want to design something a little more sophisticated. The following stamina exercises are systems used by current memory champions, which will expand your working memory and allow you to hold up to nine digits per file – or, potentially, even more.

Your working memory has to work slightly harder for this and a lot of effort has to be put in up front so that encoding and decoding are minimal. With a system that allowed you to store nine digits per file, you would have to use 100 files to remember 900 digits. However, with these types of systems current champions are memorizing more than 2,000 digits in an hour.

30-minute numbers

If you choose this as one of your stamina workouts in the next seven days, use your current system and take 30 minutes to memorize as many digits as possible. Use the same scoring as in the five-minute number workout.

Probably the most accessible version is to use your current number system and create a person, action and object for each number. For example:

▶ If 22 is a nun (person), you may imagine her praying (action) and holding a cross (object).
▶ If 44 is a lion (person), you may imagine it striking (action) with its sharp claws (object).
▶ If 20 is a NASA spaceman (person), you may imagine him flying (action) the shuttle (object).

If you bring these six digits together, you get:

A nun 22 (person) striking 44 (action) a shuttle 20 (object)

This system takes some time and effort and it is probably only really useful if you intend to compete or you need a powerful number system.

```
7  9  7  1  8  4  1  5  3  0  5  5  9  0  2  2  9  8  2  0
2  9  9  6  2  4  9  6  9  8  6  6  8  0  9  2  2  4  9  8
2  6  7  0  1  4  6  1  5  0  9  4  7  7  4  8  9  2  2  6
3  9  2  7  5  0  0  7  9  5  1  6  0  6  5  5  8  9  6  7
8  2  6  0  6  4  6  6  0  2  3  6  8  2  7  4  1  9  5  4
5  9  6  9  8  6  0  0  1  3  6  9  1  0  3  9  7  5  1  2
7  3  8  1  4  5  0  9  8  8  1  0  3  2  2  6  0  3  4  5
6  4  8  4  1  2  2  6  2  0  0  4  2  0  9  2  3  1  4  4
6  3  6  0  0  5  1  9  0  1  3  2  8  6  2  8  8  7  8  1
9  4  6  5  8  2  6  3  4  2  2  5  7  6  1  9  2  5  8  6
2  8  2  5  1  3  1  2  9  4  5  6  7  0  2  7  7  4  4  0
6  9  9  8  6  0  2  8  2  7  3  5  8  4  0  1  9  9  1  3
8  9  8  9  6  3  2  9  5  4  8  5  1  9  0  4  7  8  3  3
8  9  7  9  2  6  8  2  2  7  5  4  4  4  7  4  6  8  6  5
8  4  2  9  9  8  3  0  9  8  7  3  3  5  6  2  8  7  1  3
6  7  2  4  2  3  7  0  3  5  9  0  0  3  7  6  5  2  0  6
4  3  7  9  0  6  7  3  5  7  3  3  0  3  9  5  8  2  6  1
8  4  3  2  1  3  6  7  4  7  4  2  4  5  4  6  1  2  1  1
5  3  0  8  9  0  0  6  8  2  8  0  0  1  7  1  8  4  7  3
9  0  6  6  4  8  1  8  7  5  3  9  6  7  3  6  2  6  9  7
```

30-minute cards

This game is similar to the five-minute number workout. To begin with, set yourself up with three packs of cards. Make sure each pack is kept separate.

▶ Start the timer.
▶ Memorize as many cards as you can in 30 minutes.

20 foreign words

Building your vocabulary in a different language is a great way of challenging your creative memorization skills, giving meaning to words that initially have no meaning.

▶ Go to http://www.memrise.com

▶ Choose a language.

▶ Follow the online instructions, aiming to memorize up to 20 words.

▶ Memrise will guide you and test your recall.

MEMORIZING SPEECHES AND SCRIPTS

A great way to improve your memory for scripts or speeches on a regular basis or to learn something of interest to use in social or business situations is to use an online speech or presentation, such as one of the many TED Talks. To memorize a speech or talk, think back to Exercise 49, Using quotes, in which the key ingredients were:

▶ your **intent**

▶ the **meaning**

▶ any **emotions**

▶ **physical** actions

▶ creative **visual cues.**

Once you have those in place:

▶ prepare the words in your own language

▶ add in the words in their language

▶ cook it up for the appropriate amount of time

▶ serve with gusto!

Use this simple recipe to memorize a speech, even quite a long and complex one. Remember that you first need to extract the intent, meaning and emotions. From this you can derive the physical actions and visual cues, which will accelerate the rate at which you can recite the speech.

By preparing it in your own words, using your visual cues to hone the actual words in the script and then rehearsing it, taking a SAVI approach, you will soon improve your ability to serve up speeches, building your general knowledge at the same time.

Exercise 99

THE SPEECH

To improve your memory for scripts or to learn something of interest to use in social or business situations, it's useful to practise memorizing speeches or talks. The following workout asks you to memorize Einstein's speech, 'Peace in the atomic era', from 1950. Other options are to use an essay or find something online, such as Ken Robinson's talk 'How schools kill creativity', one of many witty, intelligent and inspirational TED Talks.

To memorize the following speech by Einstein, remember the tips for memorizing given on the previous page. Use them to memorize as much of the speech as you can in 30 minutes. When you use your visual cues, project them into your iMind, to help you remain present and in the moment.

To get you started, here are some visual cues for the first three paragraphs:

- ▶ express, conviction, political question
- ▶ security, armament, illusion
- ▶ fostered atomic bomb, superiority
- ▶ opponent intimidated, security, desired, humanity
- ▶ maxim, following five, superior military power, whatever the cost

You can easily create five images that represent these keywords, chain them together and project them on to your iMind, as follows:

'Imagine an express train moving with conviction holding a political question, it takes you to a secure armament which is just an illusion. Inside is a fostered atomic bomb that is very superior. It has an opponent who is intimidated holding a security blanket and desiring to be human. His name is Max and follows the number 5 who is determined to achieve superior military power, whatever the cost.'

Of course, this takes much longer to write out than it does just to see it in your mind, and there is no need to write out the keywords separately or as a story. Simply look at the speech, chaining visual cues as you go.

To use this speech for your workout, set your timer for 30 minutes. Good luck!

'Peace in the atomic era'

I am grateful to you for the opportunity to express my conviction in this most important political question.

The idea of achieving security through national armament is, at the present state of military technique, a disastrous illusion. On the part of the United States this illusion has been particularly fostered by the fact that this country succeeded first in producing an atomic bomb. The belief seemed to prevail that in the end it were possible to achieve decisive military superiority.

In this way, any potential opponent would be intimidated, and security, so ardently desired by all of us, brought to us and all of humanity. The maxim which we have been following during these last five years has been, in short: security through superior military power, whatever the cost.

This mechanistic, technical-military psychological attitude had inevitable consequences. Every single act in foreign policy is governed exclusively by one viewpoint.

How do we have to act in order to achieve utmost superiority over the opponent in case of war? Establishing military bases at all possible strategically important points on the globe. Arming and economic strengthening of potential allies.

Within the country – concentration of tremendous financial power in the hands of the military, militarization of the youth, close supervision of the loyalty of the citizens, in particular, of the civil servants by a police force growing more conspicuous every day. Intimidation of people of independent political thinking. Indoctrination of the public by radio, press, school. Growing restriction of the range of public information under the pressure of military secrecy.

The armament race between the USA. and the USSR, originally supposed to be a preventive measure, assumes hysterical character. On both sides, the means to mass destruction are perfected with feverish haste – behind the respective walls of secrecy. The H-bomb appears on the public horizon as a probably attainable goal. Its accelerated development has been solemnly proclaimed by the President.

If successful, radioactive poisoning of the atmosphere and hence annihilation of any life on earth has been brought within the range of technical possibilities. The ghostlike character of this development lies in its apparently compulsory trend. Every step appears as the unavoidable consequence of the preceding one. In the end, there beckons more and more clearly general annihilation.

Is there any way out of this impasse created by man himself? All of us, and particularly those who are responsible for the attitude of the US and the USSR., should realize that we may have vanquished an external enemy, but have been incapable of getting rid of the mentality created by the war.

It is impossible to achieve peace as long as every single action is taken with a possible future conflict in view. The leading point of view of all political action should therefore be: What can we do to bring about a peaceful co-existence and even loyal co-operation of the nations?

The first problem is to do away with mutual fear and distrust. Solemn renunciation of violence (not only with respect to means of mass destruction) is undoubtedly necessary. Such renunciation, however, can only be effective if at the same time a supra-national judicial and executive body is set up, empowered to decide questions of immediate concern to the security of the nations. Even a declaration of the nations to collaborate loyally in the realization of such a 'restricted world government' would considerably reduce the imminent danger of war.

In the last analysis, every kind of peaceful co-operation among men is primarily based on mutual trust and only secondly on institutions such as courts of justice and police. This holds for nations as well as for individuals. And the basis of trust is loyal give and take.

What about international control? Well, it may be of secondary use as a police measure. But it may be wise to overestimate its importance. The times of prohibition come to mind and give one pause.

PLANNING YOUR STAMINA WORKOUTS

Think about each of the stamina workouts and choose which ones you believe you can commit to over the next seven days along with your memory warm-up and speed workouts. Again, add this to your table.

After the first seven days you can either continue to create your workouts week by week or design something a little bit more flexible, as described in the next exercise.

 *Exercise 100*

BRINGING VARIETY TO YOUR WORKOUT

Here is the menu of all the exercises described in this chapter. Use it to set up a different workout every day, by randomly selecting from the list.

Use the table either as it appears here or write the name of each workout on a separate card, ideally colour coded as warm-up, speed and stamina. Then simply deal out a different selection of workouts every day, from each of those areas. This way, you will always have a variety of workouts.

Warm-ups	Speed games	Stamina games
Energize	Five-minute words	30-minute numbers
N-Back	Five-minute numbers	30-minute cards
Story cubes	Five-minute cards	20 foreign words
Recognition drills	Five-minute names	The speech
Relativistic training	Top five stories	
Metaphors	Quote of the day	
	Top three tracks	

Alternatively, you can get a pack of custom cards from:

www.achieve-with.me/memoryworkbook

Summary

In this chapter you have experienced a range of memory workouts, from warm-ups to speed games and stamina events. You have designed your next seven days in such a way that it is realistic and achievable for you to build your mastery of creative memorization. You also have a flexible workout strategy in place that will give you variety and keep you in top memory shape.

What I have learned

What are my thoughts, feelings and insights on what I have read so far?

_____

_____

_____

Use the space below to summarize the actions to take as a result of reading this chapter.

_____

_____

_____

_____

Where to next?

The final chapter will leave you with a recipe for ongoing learning, an understanding of how to build on your success and suggestions for how to continue on your journey to 'learn – grow – achieve'.

13 *Apply your memory skills*

▶ how to create your memory timeline
▶ how to understand the success cycle
▶ how to put your recipe for learning into practice.

In this chapter you will focus on applying your skills in the real world. With the goals you put in place in Chapter 1 and having completed the exercises in this workbook, you have set yourself up for ongoing success in all areas of your life.

While the previous chapter was about keeping your memory fit, this one will support you in bringing real value into your life. It will allow you to take the strategies you learned throughout the previous 'memory smarts' chapters and not only put them into action but make them a part of everything you do. You will effortlessly put your skills to use in a way that is natural and gives you results, optimizing an approach that uses 'whole-brain thinking' as a smarter way of learning.

> 'Logic will get you from A to B. Imagination will take you everywhere.'
>
> Albert Einstein

→ Your memory timeline

A memory timeline is a simple low-tech tool that you can use in conjunction with the world mind map and user stories you created in Chapter 1. Whereas the world mind map and user stories give you a picture of what you want to do and why you want to do it, the memory timeline creates the picture of *when* you will do it.

Let us think back to Jill's world map and user stories from Chapter 1 and see how she uses them with the memory timeline.

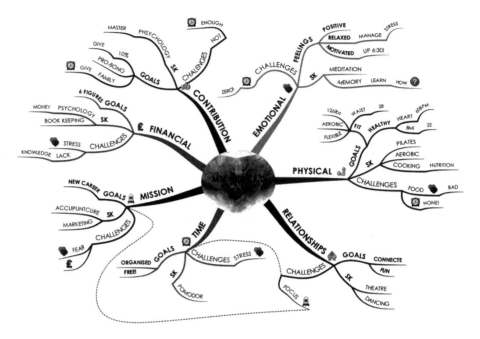

Jill's world map

Jill's five user stories

AS A successful businesswoman

I WANT TO learn…

▶ techniques to manage my stress levels

▶ how to better organize my time

▶ how to feel good about being healthy and fit

▶ how to move forward one specific area of my business (accelerate acupuncture knowledge)

▶ how to overcome any fears about my business.

Jill can choose how she wants to tackle each of the five points in this user story and plan it out on her memory timeline.

The memory timeline follows basic road-mapping principles used in product and project management. It is simple to use and you can set it up pretty much anywhere – on a wall, a window, a large whiteboard – the choice is entirely up to you. The timeline, as you might expect, represents a period of time to be defined by you. For Jill's example, let us say it is 12 months. You then chunk your timeline up into the following three parts.

1 **Ice (the next 3 months)**

This represents stories you are going to tackle first. They are solid and not likely to change.

2 **Water (3–6 months)**

The stories you plan to tackle here are more fluid and may be open to change. Like water, you will adapt and go with the flow.

3 **Steam (6–12 months)**

These stories are out there in the air, likely to change as you learn and grow, but they give you a direction in line with your world mind map.

The illustration below shows Jill's world map and memory timeline on a whiteboard, using sticky notes to hold the user stories. Each of the stories includes tasks to complete. This is a quick, easy and flexible way for Jill to add new stories and tasks when she needs to. If something is no longer relevant, she simply rips it up and throws it away. The fact that she now has a long-term vision in the shape of her mind map, she knows what she needs to learn and is tracking her plan with the timeline, will implicitly help her to be more effective with her time and prioritize the things that are most important.

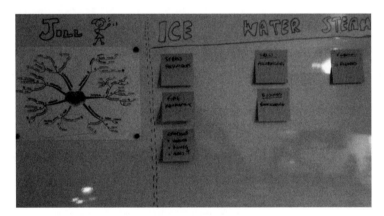

Exercise 101

CREATING YOUR TIMELINE

Take no more than 30 minutes to create some stories and actions from your world mind map and use the space here to plan out your Ice – Water – Steam memory timeline for the next 12 months.

→ Ice

_____

_____

_____

→ Water

_____

_____

_____

→ Steam

_____

_____

_____

Take a moment to really study your mind map and your timeline.
As you look at them, make a mark on the scale below to show your
level of commitment:

1_____10

If you are less than an 8, what do you need to do to raise your level
of commitment to an 8 or above?

_____

→ Success and your values

What does success in terms of learning and memory mean to you? How
will you know when you are successful? Could you describe it?

The following activity aims to uncover some of the deeper values
that are important to you in terms of learning and memory. You can
think of a value as 'what is important to you in life'. Is it relationships,
recognition, growth, contribution, family, happiness, or success for its
own sake? These are all examples of values.

Exercise 102

MEMORY AND YOUR VALUES

You will have to search your brain to discover the answers to the questions below about why memory is important to you. Here is an example of how your answers to the series of questions might go:

- ▶ Memory is important to me because it will make me feel sharper.
- ▶ If I feel sharper, I may take more in.
- ▶ If I take more in, I could progress in my role.
- ▶ If I progress in my role, I might feel I'm **growing** as a person.
- ▶ By growing as a person, I will feel more **fulfilled**.
- ▶ By feeling more fulfilled, I'll have better **relationships** with the people close to me.

You can see that, by answering these questions, you will start to uncover key values. The ones in bold above point to growth, fulfilment and relationships. By starting off with the question of why memory is important to you, you will start to uncover some of the values that drive you.

Answer the following questions as honestly as possible. Write your answers on the line provided, with each consecutive question referring to your previous answer as in the example above.

→ Why is memory important to you?

_____

→ Why is that important to you?

_____

→ What does this give you?

_____

→ Why is that important to you?

_____

→ What impact will that have on your life?

_____

→ Why is that important to you?

_____

....

→ The success cycle

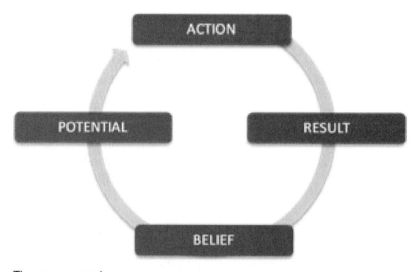

The success cycle

There are many different views of what a success cycle may look like. The one shown depicts the idea that, in order to achieve what success looks like for you, you need some supporting beliefs. These beliefs allow you to envisage your potential, which in turn leads you to take action in line with those beliefs about your potential, which will produce results that support your belief. This causes an ever-turning upward cycle that takes you towards the success you are looking for in your life, whatever that may be.

For example, let us take Jill and presume that she had a belief along the lines of 'I don't have time to do the things I want to do.' To overcome this belief, Jill creates some positive future memories that see her managing her time in a relaxed and energized manner. She makes this real for herself by 'rewiring' her brain and so supporting a new belief about her ability to manage her time better.

This new belief may be along the lines of, 'I have as much time as I allow myself to have.' This puts Jill in a position of certainty and – rather than shutting down options – it supports her real potential. She now takes an action to reprioritize what is important to her and gets a good result, which supports the new belief. If the result isn't what she is looking for, the belief can still hold true. She may need to allow herself more time, but it is still all within her control.

If you think about success and learning, you may start to see some connections. What similarities do you see between the learning and success cycle when you look at them side by side?

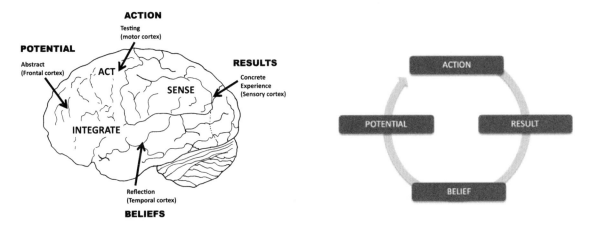

The learning cycle and the success cycle compared

If we were to take the view that memories of experiences can influence our beliefs and therefore the decisions and actions we ultimately take, we see how important it is that we are aware of how our memories are guiding us, either towards or away from the success we are looking for in our lives. In this sense, we have the choice of whether a past or future memory is useful to us. Since we have the skills to 'create memories', we have the skill to create beliefs that support us.

MEMORY BELIEFS

What beliefs are currently holding you back from experiencing the success you are looking for in your life in line with your values?

In the table below, write down three beliefs that hold you back or don't support you in some way. Then think about how you could creatively reshape that belief to one that would be in line with your values and support you in the direction you wish to go.

Limiting belief	Empowering belief
1	1
2	2
3	3

What future memories could you now create that would support your new empowering beliefs?

Make visual notes in the space below, sketching out a simple picture for each belief. Make the memory as real as possible, remembering the affective memory exercises. The more 'real' and emotional you can make it, the easier it will be to integrate this new learning.

Once you have experienced this memory with crystal clarity, you need to test it out. Decide on what action you can take that will allow you to realize your new potential.

Include this in your visual notes below.

→ Recipe for learning

In Exercise 39, Designing your learning, you used Meier's SAVI principles and rapid instructional design to design and share an experience around creative memorization, the chain method and a memory network with a friend. Meir also offers a simple menu to pull these principles together. The idea of creative memorization fits nicely into this menu. Whether you are designing training for a group, your children or yourself, the menu guides you step by step.

1 Preparation: start by getting clear on your goals, outcomes and benefits.

2 Presentation: get straight into your main dish – these are your SAVI activities and where creative memorization can come into play.

3 Practice: set up your appetizers – these are activites to arouse, raise interest and spark curiosity, heightening engagement with the learning experience.

4 Performance: prepare your dessert – these are activities that test skills and knowledge and prepare you for the real world.

YOUR FINAL CHALLENGE

As a final challenge and to consolidate your learning, use the recipe for learning to capture the highlights of this workbook. Create a session you can share with someone else that offers them skills they can put into practice in a real-world situation.

Follow this menu and create your session in whatever form feels right in the space below.

Summary

Congratulations on completing this workbook! Through more than 100 exercises, you have expanded your thinking, designed your own training programme and created a plan to incorporate your new skills into your personal and professional life, in order to achieve your goals.

What I have learned

What are my thoughts, feelings and insights on what I have read so far?

_____

_____

_____

Use the space below to summarize the actions to take as a result of reading this chapter.

_____

_____

_____

_____

Where to next?

As you have seen, the final stage of the recipe for learning is performance. During this phase it is important that you put what you have learned into practice in real-life situations. In terms of this workbook, this is where you are right now. You have the toolbox at your fingertips to learn anything, increase your skills and achieve your goals.

Quick help

A whole set of resources is available online at
www.achieve-with.me

Whether you use this space to monitor your progress, share and
get tips from the community or take the next step into training or
coaching, achieve-with.me is there to offer you ongoing support
as you continue your journey.

The Memory Workbook Facebook group

Finally, join the community of people improving their memory and
achieving results, ask questions, get help, share challenges and
successes. This is a great community where you can get advice
and tips as you go through this workbook, as well as invitations
to free webinars with Mark Channon Coaching and first-hand
advice on improving your skills.

http://www.facebook.com/groups/memory-workbook

You are about to embark on a fun and exciting journey that can
deliver some powerful benefits. Enjoy!

References

BIBLIOGRAPHY

Armstrong, T., *7 kinds of smart* (New York: Plume, 1999)

Baddeley, A.D., & Hitch, G., 'Working memory' in Bower, G.H. (ed.), *The psychology of learning and motivation: Advances in research and theory* (Vol. 8, pp. 47–89) (New York: Academic Press, 1974)

Byrne, J. (ed.), *Concise Learning and Memory* (Waltham, Mass.: Academic Press, 2009)

Engeser, S., *Advances in Flow Research* (Berlin: Springer, 2012)

Foer, J., *Moonwalking with Einstein* (London: Penguin, 2011)

Gardner, H., *Frames of Mind: The Theory of Multiple Intelligences* (New York: Basic Books, 2011)

Goleman, D., *Emotional Intelligence* (New York: Bantam Books, 1995)

Goleman, D., *Working with Emotional Intelligence* (London: Bloomsbury, 1998)

Gordon, M., *The Stanislavsky Technique* (Milwaukee: Applause Theatre Book Publishers, 1988)

Kolb, D., *Experiential Learning* (Upper Saddle River, NJ, 1983)

Kroeger, O. and Thuesen, J., *Type Talk* (New York: Dell Publishing, 1988)

Masters, R.S.W., 'The role of explicit versus implicit knowledge in the breakdown of a complex motor skill under pressure' (*British Journal of Psychology*, 83: 343–58 (1992)

Meier, D., *The Accelerated Learning Handbook* (New York: McGraw-Hill, 2000)

Rhode, M., *The Sketchnote Handbook* (San Francisco: Peachpit Press, 2013)

Robbins, A., *Personal Power II* (San Diego: Robbins Research International, Inc., 2011)

Sprenger, M., *Learning and Memory* (Alexandria, VA: ASCD, 1999)

Sprenger, M., *Differentiation Through Learning Styles and Memory* (Thousand Oaks, CA: Corwin Press, 2008)

Yates, F., *The Art of Memory* (London: Pimlico, 1966)

Zull, J., *The Art of Changing the Brain* (Sterling, VA: Stylus Publishing, 2002)

WEBSITES

Roam, D., The Napkin Academy (http://www.napkinacademy.com)

Jaeggi, S. M., Buschkuehl, M., Jonides, J. and Perrig, W. J., 'Improving fluid intelligence with training on working memory' http://www.pnas.org/content/105/19/6829.full (2008).

http://www.ted.com/talks/daniel_kahneman_the_riddle_of_experience_vs_memory.html

The World Memory Sports Council

http://www.worldmemorychampionships.com/absolutecontent/content/files/Memory_Disciplines.pdf

www.achieve-with.me/memoryworkbook

http://www.ted.com/talks/ken_robinson_says_schools_kill_creativity.html

'Mind Map' is a registered trademark of the Buzan Organization Ltd 1990, www.thinkbuzan.com

Exercise 7 adapted from Tony Robbins, Personal Power (audio CD); listen online: www.achieve-with.me/the-memory-workbook/

Exercise 45: http://www.readingfirst.virginia.edu/elibrary_pdfs/Building_Vocabulary.pdf

Exercise 46: http://www.businessballs.com/business-dictionary.htm

Exercise 68: http://www.everyhit.com

Exercise 92: names and faces used with permission from the World Memory Sports Council, www.worldmemorysportscouncil.com

Success cycle diagram in Chapter 13 from Anthony Robbins, www.tonyrobbins.com/products/personal.../personal-power-2.php

Index